THE
CULTURALLY
PROFICIENT
School

THE CULTURALLY PROFICIENT School

An Implementation Guide for School Leaders

Randall B. Lindsey 🖉 Laraine M. Roberts
Franklin CampbellJones

CORWIN PRESS
A Sage Publications Company
Thousand Oaks, California

For information:

Corwin Press
A Sage Publications Company
2455 Teller Road
Thousand Oaks,
California 91320
www.corwinpress.com

Sage Publications Ltd.
1 Oliver's Yard
55 City Road
London EC1Y 1SP
United Kingdom

Sage Publications India Pvt. Ltd.
B-42, Panchsheel Enclave
Post Box 4109
New Delhi 110 017 India

Printed in the United States of America

Library of Congress Cataloging-in-Publication Data

Lindsey, Randall B.
The culturally proficient school: an implementation guide for school leaders / by
Randall B. Lindsey, Laraine M. Roberts, Franklin CampbellJones.
　　　p. cm.
Includes bibliographical references and index.
ISBN 13: 978-0-7619-4681-6 (cloth)—ISBN 13: 978-0-7619-4682-3 (pbk.)
　　1. Multicultural education—United States—Case studies. 2. School
improvement programs—United States—Case studies. 3. Educational
leadership—United States—Case studies. I. Roberts, Laraine M.
II. CampbellJones, Franklin. III. Title.
LC1099.3.L557 2005
370.117—dc22   2004007963

This book is printed on acid-free paper.

　　　　　　　　　　07　　08　10　 9　 8　 7　 6　 5　 4

Acquisitions Editor:	Rachel Livsey
Editorial Assistant:	Phyllis Cappello
Production Editor:	Julia Parnell
Copy Editor:	Dan Hays
Typesetter/Designer:	C&M Digitals (P) Ltd.
Proofreader:	Carla Freeman
Indexer:	Jean Casalegno
Cover Designer:	Tracy E. Miller
Production Artist:	Anthony Paular

Contents

Foreword

School administrators facing issues of accountability, diversity, and no child left behind expectations may benefit from a work that presents a process by which to respond to these challenges. The process is not a quick fix, recipe, or the answer to serious issues. However, the process does address questions such as the following: How culturally proficient am I? How culturally proficient is my school? What are the stages by which I and my school become culturally proficient? How can I tell if we are making progress? How is this proficiency related to the relationships I need to develop and sustain? How do these relationships and our cultural proficiency relate to our accountability to our constituents? How is cultural proficiency linked to the improvement of student performance?

The Culturally Proficient School focuses on cultural proficiency as a concept that calls for school leaders to respond to the challenges facing them in their schools and communities. The issue of differences in the school organization is dealt with from the standpoint of the leaders. These differences are conceived as cultural, which call for some response that may consist of six stages: cultural destructiveness, cultural incapacity, cultural blindness, cultural precompetence, cultural competence, and cultural proficiency. These stages range from purging cultures to honoring differences among cultures. Leader behaviors, values, and attitudes are dealt with to illustrate how culturally proficient leaders succeed in bringing about improvement in student performance.

This book is a friendly invitation to consider and try certain strategies to improve the culture of schools and to become culturally proficient. A valuable contribution of this work is that the responsibility for the betterment of schools is firmly lodged on the leadership of the organization as well as others. Cultural proficiency is a type of relationship that exists between the leader and others but also between members of the organization and community. How that relationship is developed, nurtured, and strengthened is systematically presented.

As an instructional strategy, the use of the Maple View case and the practical "how to" chapters are particularly effective. The case presents a picture of reality we have all experienced, whereas the "how to, can do" chapters reflect a spirit of optimism and well-crafted strategies to help leaders and others to develop cultural proficiency. This is not a simple step-by-step description of assuming attitudes, behaviors, and values advocated by the authors as consisting of cultural proficiency. Instead, it is a work that demands reflection, experimentation, and insight into organizational and personal aspects of associating with one another.

Inasmuch as the authors express modest intentions of this book, the value of this work for me lies in the clarity of the relationship between the case, the conceptual framework, and the call for leadership and organizational purpose. It is rare to find a work that is pragmatic, data based, and theoretically sound with the potential to not only impact the preparation of school leaders but also elevate the possibilities for our schools and youth.

Flora Ida Ortiz
University of California, Riverside

Acknowledgments

Terry L. Cross (1989) and colleagues, Barbara J. Barzon, Karl W. Dennis, and Mareasa R. Isaacs, provided a gift to our society with their seminal monograph *Toward a Culturally Competent System of Care*. The framework they developed offers sensitive and responsive ways to meet the needs of culturally and ethnically diverse clients and serves as an effective tool for those concerned with making preschool through Grade 12 schools, colleges, and universities attentive to the needs and desires of our diverse constituencies.

This book is the third in a series inspired by Cross and colleagues. Randall B. Lindsey collaborated with Kikanza Nuri Robins and Raymond D. Terrell to write *Cultural Proficiency: A Manual for School Leaders* (1999, 2003). Delores B. Lindsey joined Nuri Robins, Lindsey, and Terrell to write *Culturally Proficient Instruction: A Guide for People Who Teach* (2002). We are most appreciative of their in-depth work that demonstrates for educators how to apply cultural proficiency in school settings. Their work has set a new standard for educators willing to educate all children and youth. With this book, the team of educators working with the construct of cultural proficiency widens. We draw from the concepts developed by Cross et al., Lindsey et al., and Nuri Robins et al. and add the voices that we are hearing from our colleagues in preschool through Grade 12 schools, colleges, and universities.

This book is about voice. The three of us have, cumulatively, several decades of experience with P–12, college, and university education. During our careers, beginning in the early 1960s, public education has expanded to serve ever-widening sectors of society. At best, it has been uneven, and at worst it has contributed to the disparities in our society. Our goal in writing this book is to provide a handbook for the many educational leaders we encounter who are seeking opportunities to have meaningful conversations about developing culturally proficient practices.

We are deeply indebted to our many generous colleagues who have supported us in this work. There are many people represented in these pages as the voices to whom we have listened and from whom we have learned. They are the voices of teachers, teacher aides, administrators, parents, community members, and college and university faculty who have an abiding interest in our schools being ever more successful in serving the academic and social needs of our children and youth. We have labored with one another in the creation of this book. Our labor ends with a sense that we have only begun the process of telling the story of what cultural proficiency looks like in practice.

We appreciatively thank James Crow for his dedicated and tireless editing of our work and for his extraordinary commitment to helping us complete our project by consistently giving us constructive and encouraging feedback. Our respect and love also go to Delores Lindsey, who has been a supporter of this work from its preproposal stage and who has provided strong support, affection, and critical feedback at all stages of development. Also, we are truly grateful for the loving enthusiasm, friendship, and critical feedback that Brenda CampbellJones has given us as this project moved from conception to near-completed drafts. Jim, Delores, and Brenda are professional partners, as well as partners for life, in this important work of serving the needs of our diverse communities. Our editor, Rachel Livsey, has been a true friend of this project and ours. Her suggestions, perspectives, and unflagging encouragement were instrumental in the development and completion of this project.

The contributions of the following reviewers are gratefully acknowledged:

Susan Kessler, Ed.D.
Assistant Principal
Metro Nashville Public Schools
Nashville, TN

Elaine L. Wilmore, Ph.D.
Associate Professor of Educational Leadership and Policy Studies
    and Special Assistant to the Dean
University of Texas at Arlington
Arlington, TX

Philip Collis McCullum
Director, Administrator Licensure Programs
Director, Institute for Leadership and Diversity in Education
University of Oregon
College of Education
Eugene, OR

Ronald L. Russell
Assessment Consultant
Loess Hills Area Education Agency 13
Atlantic, IA

Stephanie Graham
Consultant
Los Angeles County Office of Education
Downey, CA

About the Authors

Randall B. Lindsey, PhD, is Principal Associate of The Robins Group. He is Professor Emeritus at California State University, Los Angeles, where he served as chair of the Division of Administration and Counseling in the School of Education. He has served as a junior and senior high school teacher of history and as an administrator of school desegregation and staff development programs. He has worked extensively with school districts as they plan for and experience changing populations. Lindsey and his wife, Delores, live in Orange, California, where they enjoy the unique pleasures of living in southern California. (randalllinbdsey@aol.com)

Laraine M. Roberts, EdD, is Senior Research Associate at WestEd in San Francisco. Her work centers on educational leadership, organizational culture, and school and district development and improvement. In addition to leading educational research projects, she designs and facilitates leadership development programs for superintendents, district administrators, and school principals. In all her work, her goal is to influence changes within the structures of schools and the practices of educators that result in meaningful learning experiences and academic success for all students. Her experiences as an educator include classroom teaching, school and district administration, professional development, curriculum development, and university teaching.

Franklin CampbellJones, EdD, is Associate Professor of Education Leadership at Rowan University in Glassboro, New Jersey. He completed 6 years as a tenured faculty member of education leadership at California State University, Los Angeles. He is a national and international facilitator of organization learning and diversity. His 30-year service in education includes tenure as a high school social science teacher, school administrator, and project director for the State of California. (Campbelljones1@aol.com)

For
Delores, Kikanza, and Ray for their loving guidance.

With loving appreciation to Laura Boucher because she always expected the best and to James Crow, who patiently continues the tradition.

Julia Mae Jones, whose life was a narrative illustration of the essence of this book, and Brenda CampbellJones, who continues in that tradition.

Introduction

*The school must allow cultural elements that
are relevant to the children to enter the
classroom . . . thereby enabling the child to move
through relevant experiences from the home
toward the demands of the school as
representative of [a diverse] society . . . We must
first comprehend the fact that children—all
children—come to school motivated to enlarge
their culture. But we must start with their
culture . . . and look first to determine how they
seek to know themselves and others and how their
expertise and experience can be used as the fuel to
fire their interests, knowledge, and skills . . . for
they are rich in assets. As teachers, we enter their
world in order to aid them and to build bridges
between two cultures.*

—Eugene Garcia (1999, p. 82)

What if we were to think of schooling as building bridges between cultures? In addition, what if we were to envision education as a means of enlarging one's own culture through meaningful interactions with people from other cultures? What then would we see in our schools and classrooms? Quite possibly we would see educators searching for ways to work more successfully with students who represent the many different cultural, ethnic, linguistic, religious, and economic subcultures within our diverse society. Cultural and social diversity is certainly not a new issue facing us as humans. It has always existed, and we remain challenged by it. However, the burgeoning complexity of our times calls upon us as educators to face this challenge more directly, to value diversity, honor it with integrity, and to preserve the cultural dignity of our students.

Failing this test places far too many of our students at a serious disadvantage of being excluded from the benefits and opportunities of being well educated. This book addresses the challenges that grow out of the demographic array of students we serve in our schools by offering an approach to education that embraces diversity and responds to it in ways that acknowledge and esteem cultural differences while simultaneously valuing and supporting similarities in a process of additive rather than subtractive acculturation (Ogbu, 1992). The approach we propose is cultural proficiency, which offers both educators and their students knowledge and understanding of how to interact effectively with people in their environments who differ from them. The cultural proficiency model we describe derives from the work of Terry Cross in a monograph he wrote for health care practitioners, *Toward a Culturally Competent System of Care* (Cross, 1989; Cross, Bazron, Dennis, & Isaacs, 1993).

"Cultural proficiency?" "What is that?" "What does it mean?" Some of the educators with whom we work ask these questions when we introduce the term. Quite often, their follow-up questions reveal their real concerns about expected behaviors: "What does it look like in practice?" Commonly, the unspoken concerns are, "Will I be expected to change my behavior?" "Will I have to act differently?" and "What if I feel uncomfortable?" Other educators immediately begin to find ways to integrate new practices into their interactions with students. They want to work more effectively with students who represent the many different cultural groups within our diverse society. Whereas some search for quick fixes that do not exist, others understand the systemic nature of cultural change in an organization and begin the complex work of transforming their schools and districts into inclusive communities whose members view acknowledgment and respect for diverse groups as appropriate and worthy goals for their organizations.

Organizational change is challenging and requires a leader's persistent systemic reinforcement. Indeed, Edgar Schein, in *Organizational Culture and Leadership* (1992), emphatically argues that "the only thing of real importance that leaders do is create and manage culture and . . . the unique talent of leaders is their ability to understand and work with culture" (p. 5).

Educational leaders intent on transforming their schools and districts into pluralistic, inclusive organizations must first be willing and able to look deeply into their own tacit assumptions about the diverse students with whom they work and examine their expectations about those students' achievement potential. Leaders also must identify and pursue effective ways to educate all their students successfully, using strategies that both acknowledge and respond to the students' varied cultural backgrounds. This book offers ideas, tools, and processes that will serve as a guide for leaders through the complex and challenging cultural transformation of their organizations. Again, Schein's (1992) work illuminates this idea:

> I believe that cultures begin with leaders who impose their own values and assumptions on a group. If that group is successful and the [leader's] assumptions come to be taken for granted, we have then a culture that will define for later generations of members what kinds of leadership are acceptable. The culture now defines leadership. But, as the group encounters adaptive difficulties, as its environment changes to the point where some of its assumptions are no longer valid, leadership comes into play once more. Leadership now is the ability to step outside the culture that created the leader and to start evolutionary changes that are more adaptive. This ability to perceive the limitations of one's own culture and to develop the culture adaptively is the essence and ultimate challenge of leadership. (pp. 1–2)

In this book, our goal is to share with you what we are learning from our work with leaders who recognize the disparities in our schools and who have made a commitment to leverage their leadership to create and manage schools and districts that function at high levels of cultural and social interaction among diverse groups. These leaders acknowledge that diversity is far more than racial or ethnic differences, and their actions reflect a sincere intent to understand and respond to all the subgroups in their schools and districts—particularly groups other than the ones they represent. These leaders also recognize that responses and reactions to cultural diversity have a profound influence on what students learn and how they learn it. Moreover, they have learned that responding to and reacting to *difference* manifest in several ways, which range from cultural destructiveness to cultural proficiency. The range of these responses comprises the points of the cultural proficiency continuum (Lindsey, Nuri Robins, & Terrell, 1999, 2003):

- *Cultural destructiveness:* negating, disparaging, or purging cultures that are different from your own
- *Cultural incapacity:* elevating the superiority of your own cultural values and beliefs and suppressing cultures that are different from your own
- *Cultural blindness:* acting as if differences among cultures do not exist and refusing to recognize any differences

- *Cultural precompetence:* recognizing that lack of knowledge, experience, and understanding of other cultures limits your ability to effectively interact with them
- *Cultural competence:* interacting with other cultural groups in ways that recognize and value their differences, motivate you to assess your own skills, expand your knowledge and resources, and, ultimately, cause you to adapt your relational behavior
- *Cultural proficiency:* honoring the differences among cultures, viewing diversity as a benefit, and interacting knowledgeably and respectfully among a variety of cultural groups

We believe that pluralistic and democratic schooling is possible and that education leaders can create cultures in which cultural proficiency is a dominant value. Schools in which these ideals take root and flourish require leaders to both model and expect behaviors that are consistent with them. Through our work, we have observed that schools begin to change when their leaders recognize the disparities that exist in our schools and then intentionally raise issues of bias, preference, legitimization, privilege, and equity. By choosing to face these issues and grapple with them directly to understand their effects on student learning, these leaders are moving their schools and districts toward culturally proficient practices. However, if they choose to turn away from these issues as if they have no effect on student learning, then, of course, nothing will change. In these circumstances, the achievement gap between students who experience privilege and entitlement and the students who do not will continue to grow and deepen. It is our choice as educators: We can contribute to the gap, or we can challenge and change the contextual conditions that support the inequities that created and perpetuate the academic achievement gap.

Our Invitation to You

As you read this book, we invite you to consider new or alternative perspectives on the many ways we can educate the diverse groups of students in our schools and classrooms. The approach we propose is a focused strategy that significantly and persistently addresses the problems of educational inequity. We firmly believe that education leaders must mobilize a sustained and coherent strategy that challenges the dominant deficit and at-risk characterizations of some students. An inclusive, pluralistic, and instructionally powerful learning environment offers the real likelihood that all students will be well-educated and successful learners.

Education leaders who pursue the goals of pluralistic and democratic schooling act intentionally with the belief that all children and youth not only have the capacity to learn but also are learning something about themselves and others at every moment. Although these democratic educators would acknowledge that most U.S. schools are very successful in the work of educating the students for whom they were designed, they recognize that this designated group is a narrow, unicultural cluster of students who represent the mainstream European American individualistic values that dominate public education in the United States. Furthermore, these educators understand the imperative that all students must receive the caliber of education they need to fully contribute to and sustain our democratic society. Also, they remain skeptical of the conventional explanations given for the achievement gap—that there is something wrong with the student, their parents, or their culture—and are fully committed to identifying and removing deterrents to academic achievement among undereducated students.

Mainstream assumptions about what is causing the achievement gap usually identify one of two dominant perspectives. One well-documented perspective is that some children—generally poor children of color and children who have language "liabilities"—are not succeeding in our schools. The second perspective—equally well documented—is that systems of oppression, such as racism and exclusion, are responsible for the undereducation, if not the miseducation, of many students—again, generally poor children of color and children who have language limitations (Delpit, 1995; Ladson-Billings, 1994; Nieto, 2000). We certainly agree with these two perspectives and discuss them in this book because they help shape an understanding of culturally proficient practices. However, we also include a third perspective that describes how children and youth for whom our schools were designed and for whom they function well—generally students from mainstream ethnic, social, and economic groups—also experience deficits. Their worldview of privilege and entitlement excludes and isolates them from learning how to interact effectively in a multicultural society in which their values are but one facet. We examine these three perspectives and describe how they intersect in U.S. educational practices and institutions. An important purpose of our work is to describe how systems of oppression, such as racism and exclusion, obstruct the educational progress of some students while they simultaneously benefit and propel the progress of other students. Traditional views of educational racism and exclusion often focus on their obstructive effects (Kovel, 1984; Terry, 1970). Our book offers leadership strategies that are sensitive to how and why some children and youth fail in our schools and why—and at what cost—others succeed. We invite you on this journey to find the will and means for our schools to serve the educational needs of all students.

Our Intent

Our intent is to weave a tapestry of strategies with an understanding of organizations as dynamic and culturally adaptive systems that can significantly support transformative learning—what educational journalist Gene Maeroff (1999) describes as "altered destinies." A central tenet of this book is that effective leaders act with intentions informed through a personal transformation of taking responsibility to lead in a way that addresses the educational needs of all students (Delpit, 1995; Ladson-Billings, 1994; Reeves, 2000).

Part I is composed of Chapter 1, which introduces the case story and the importance of culturally proficient leadership. Chapter 1 begins with a vital question: Why is culturally proficient leadership important? This chapter introduces a case story that we intertwine throughout the rest of the book as a way to illustrate the complexity of cultural leadership and organizational change. The case returns to the fictional town of Maple View, which was first presented in *Culturally Proficient Instruction: A Guide for People Who Teach* (Nuri Robins, Lindsey, Lindsey, & Terrell, 2002). The Maple View story involves you in the lives of people who confront the lack of inclusive equity throughout their community and schools. Through this case, we intend to illustrate the ways in which educators might experience and practice the concepts we present in this book. The Maple View story presents accounts of individuals and groups who face obstacles, such as their own cultural insensitivity and preferences, that lead to selectively biased instructional relationships, inconsistent resource allocation, uneven student accomplishment, and unequal power relationships in classrooms, schools, and the district. The story and the characters are composites of real people in real schools with whom we have worked. The case also demonstrates the ways in which the individuals and groups in Maple View overcome these deterrents through their willingness to learn and work together to become culturally proficient. Our hope is that these stories inspire your own commitment and action.

Part II consists of Chapters 2 through 5. In these chapters, we describe the features of culturally proficient educational practice and delineate the fundamental characteristics of such practice. In addition, these chapters expand the concept of cultural proficiency through the introduction of definitions, illustrations, group process exercises, and leadership tools. The activities and tools in these chapters invite you to participate in a process of reflection, and maybe transformation, of your personal leadership. In Chapters 2 through 4, you will learn the basic tools of cultural proficiency—the guiding principles, continuum, and the five essential elements. You will learn how to use these tools through vignettes reflective of real conversations other educators are having about teaching, learning, and leading. Chapter 5 leads you through an examination of barriers to personal change and organizational change. Barriers are systemic practices and policies that inhibit the learning of some children. It is our responsibility as educational leaders to adapt our practices to the needs of our students. This chapter will show you when and how people deal with their anger and guilt when confronting personal transformation.

In Part III, Chapters 6 and 7, we provide techniques leaders use to inspire organizational learning and change as strategies for achieving cultural proficiency in their schools and districts. The intent of these chapters is to focus on developing skillful leadership practices. In these chapters, we examine the importance of data-driven problem solving and propose that when leaders have the facility to use effective tools and problem-solving skills, they have the potential to bring their intentions into being. Finally, we posit that culturally proficient leaders set the tone and provide the example for those they lead. Indeed, they must be role models for the change they envision. The challenge we pose for leaders is to stay focused on the future they imagine and let that be the context for all their actions. Most important, education leaders must learn how to exemplify and generate new ways of believing and behaving that reflect pluralistic and democratic values.

The References and Bibliography provide you with the works that informed our writing in this book and are resources for you to consider when adding to your professional libraries. We wish you good fortune as you continue to find ways to meet the needs of our children and youth.

Part I

Cultural Proficiency and the Achievement Gap

1

Why Is Culturally Proficient Leadership Important?

Giving priority to what matters is the path of risk and adventure, but I also believe that the institutions and culture that surround us are waiting for us to transform them into a fuller expression of our own desires. We have the potential to reclaim and experience our freedom and put our helplessness behind us. We have the capacity to experience an intimate connection with other people and with all we come in contact with, rather than feeling that we exist in relationships born of barter and instrumentality. We also have the capacity and maturity to live a life of service and engagement, rather than the primary pursuit of entitlement and interests that focus on ourselves.

—Peter Block (2001, p. 7)

The Case: Maple View

Maple View is a growing suburban city that has expanded rapidly during the past 6 years. Two years ago, the city's population was 30,000 and included mainly middle-income and lower-salaried workers and their families. At that time, the new Pine Hills Estates development of "executive" homes was just beginning to grow and add upper-income residents. These professionals commuted from several large high-tech corporate headquarters and research and development centers in the area. It was just 2 years ago that the city's Planning and Economic Development Department estimated that the Pine Hills Estates residents represented approximately 5% of the population. At that time, middle-income residents comprised approximately 65% of the city's population and major economic base; approximately 23% of the population were low-salaried, service industry workers; and the remaining 7% were "working poor" or unemployed and dependent on government assistance for many of their basic services and family needs.

Now, 2 years later, Maple View's population has increased by more than 2,500 residents. The city's chamber of commerce has adopted the slogan, "Maple View on the Rise: Our City Is Growing to Meet Your Needs!" This growth has included additional residents in all sectors of the population. The key stimulus for this increase has been the upsurge of housing across economic segments. On the west side, the developer of the Pine Hills Estates has built an additional 150 large, expensive homes, many around a newly developed golf course. Much of this new construction has taken over land previously used for agriculture, including a popular cut-flower farm that employed 40 people throughout the year, with additional temporary workers during high-volume times. The west side has also been a growth area for new middle-class housing tracts that have drawn new residents to Maple View from more congested and densely populated urban centers. Three new, moderately priced developments have added 275 well-constructed but small homes that have sold very quickly because of their pricing. In addition, because of the master plan developed with the support of the volunteer service group, Leadership Maple View, the Planning and Economic Development Department submitted a housing development proposal to the U.S. Department of Housing and Urban Development. Maple View successfully won a federal grant and built 186 subsidized apartments and 30 low-cost houses on the east side of the city.

The city's rapid growth is exerting pressure on its social institutions, such as schools, public transit, and hospitals, while at the same time stimulating economic development of its business community. Several new retail shopping centers, banks, chain restaurants, movie theater complexes, and national chain superstores such as Home Depot, Target, and PETsMART have opened on the west side. In addition, a new upscale shopping "galleria" has replaced the old mall next to the state highway. A state-of-the-art movie multiplex is near completion next to the galleria, along with four new upscale restaurants. The city's planners are also developing construction specifications for a civic center complex that will include a new city hall, police department, and performing arts center. The specifications will go out to bid next month.

The east side, with the exception of the new low-cost housing units, is not experiencing much outside economic development. A major state highway divides Maple View into two separate communities, and few east side residents go beyond this boundary unless they are venturing to one of the large discount chain stores just across the highway. The "old" downtown, as people in the city's business community refer to it these days, is no longer the economic center of the city. Many of the original stores have gone out of business. However, new businesses, stores, and restaurants are opening in the old buildings, and they are contributing to a vibrant local economic community that offers the products and services reflecting the lifestyles and preferences of the east side residents. The city's Planning and Economic Development Department is neither investing in new development nor refurbishing the old neighborhood parks and public buildings on the east side, and the area is taking on a shabby look of disrepair in some sections. Quite a few east side homeowners in the Maple Street and Main Street sections are justifiably proud of their vintage houses and have invested a great deal of time and effort in restoring and maintaining them. In fact, many young professional couples are choosing to purchase these older homes and live in east side neighborhoods rather than in the newly built homes on the west side.

The large University Medical Center is located near the northwest city limits of Maple View. This 450-bed teaching hospital is an important source of employment for the city's residents—from doctors to janitors and from administrators to laundry workers. The hospital's chief administrative officer, Dr. Jack Bradley, has been involved in community development efforts in Maple View for the

15 years that he has worked at the hospital. As a pediatrician, he has experienced the changes in Maple View's population firsthand. In the past 5 or 6 years, he has treated an increasingly diverse group of young patients and also has observed the results of economic, cultural, social, and educational disparities. Dr. Bradley lives with his family in an older section of Maple View on the east side. As the volunteer project director for Leadership Maple View, Dr. Bradley has made it his personal mission to develop leadership capacity across his diverse community. He spearheaded the leadership group that developed the proposal for federal funding of low-cost housing in the city. He is currently working with Dr. James Harris, Director of Academic Programs at the Tri-Cities Community College (TCCC), on a new leadership effort to involve east-side residents in an innovative bilingual–bicultural medical assistant training at the hospital. The new program will be called "Culturally Proficient Medical Assistance Training."

Tri-Cities Community College is on the southeastern edge of the city, approximately 5 miles from the old downtown center. The 2-year college serves 1,900 students from Maple View and two nearby cities. Dr. Harris and other administrators at the college are concerned about the disappointing statistics they have just received as part of a report on their students' transfer to 4-year colleges and universities. Only approximately one third of their entering students complete the university transfer credits and go on to complete a 4-year degree program. The administrators at TCCC worry that many graduates from area high schools are entering the college poorly prepared to succeed in the rigorous academic program required for transfer to a 4-year degree program. Dr. Harris fears that these students not only enter TCCC poorly prepared but also have no idea how to access sufficient support and assistance to become fully prepared. He believes that these students grow to fault themselves and accept blame for not having the "cultural capital" to successfully navigate the educational system. Dr. Harris has made an appointment with Dr. Barbara Campbell, the superintendent of the Maple View School District, to discuss this issue and find ways to support the students.

■ Maple View School District

The public school system in Maple View has a great reputation. The district consistently scores in the top 15% of districts throughout the state in the statewide standardized testing program. As a result, almost all the families in the city send their children to their local, neighborhood schools. The Maple View School District serves 11,200 students from preschool through Grade 12. The ethnic composition of the student enrollment reflects the racial diversity of the city's population:

37% European American

24% Latino American (first, second, and third generation from Central America, South America, and Mexico)

21% Asian American (third and fourth generation from China and second and third generation from Korea and the Philippines)

14% African American

2% Native American

2% Pacific Islanders (first and second generation from American Samoa)

Twelve percent of the student population is in special education programs, and 10% of the students are learning English as a second language. Across the district, students speak nine different primary languages.

Dr. Barbara Campbell, in her second year as superintendent, and the members of the district's school board, along with other district administrators, recently worked together at an administrative retreat to create a statement of their vision for the district. They published the following statement: "The Maple View School District commits its effort and resources to provide a high-quality education for all students that enables each one to achieve or exceed high academic and performance standards." Dr. Campbell, or "Barbara" as she prefers to be called by her colleagues, is not completely satisfied with the negotiated statement, but she knows that she can work with it. However, she is pleased with the collaborative process used to develop the vision statement.

The growth in student enrollment is a major concern for the superintendent and the school board. In the past year, they have dealt with thorny issues of reassigning students, locating portable classrooms on school sites, and investing in new construction. Throughout this challenging period, Dr. Campbell has kept her focus on issues of equitable distribution of resources, fair and just allocation of high-quality educational experiences, and the acceleration of achievement for undereducated and underperforming students.

The school board members are elected at-large and serve the entire district rather than a particular geographical area or constituency. In elections during the past 10 years, very few east-side residents have sought office, and no one from the east-side neighborhoods has served on the board for at least 6 years. Eighteen months ago, the five current board members asked Dr. Campbell, then Assistant Superintendent of Educational Services, to consider assuming the position of district superintendent. The previous superintendent retired after 10 years in the position. Barbara agreed, and the board's vote to approve her contract was unanimous, and they assured her that she had their full support.

Recent construction and development within the district's boundaries, especially on the west side, have resulted in significant revenue growth from developer fees and real estate assessments. Dr. Campbell views these funds as resources that she can use to equalize resources across the district. She is troubled by poor student performance results in the schools in east-side neighborhoods, and she knows that those schools have fewer fully qualified teachers than schools on the west side. She also knows that many of the teachers at the east-side's Maple View Elementary School and Maple View Middle School are working with emergency credentials and are not fully prepared to teach the subject matter for their assigned grade levels or departments. Barbara's vision is to transform these schools into high-performing learning communities like the schools on the west side.

■ Maple View: The People

The story of the city of Maple View, its school district, and its residents provides an illustration of why culturally proficient leadership is important. The fictional characters in the case face many of the challenges that will confront you as a leader who is searching for ways to integrate culturally proficient attitudes and behaviors into your leadership practices. Because schools do not exist in isolation of the communities they serve, the Maple View case story allows us to present a contextualized setting in which a variety of situations occur and in which the members of this community are willing and motivated to reveal themselves and their thinking because they have problems to solve. The process of learning and solving the problems faced by characters in this case story makes known the cultural transformation that takes hold in their schools and alters the outcomes of its members. This case presents only a small sampling of the kinds of issues that might surface in an educational setting such as the Maple View School District. Nonetheless, the case offers an opportunity to analyze the actions of the characters and learn why culturally proficient leadership is so important.

You will meet many of the citizens of Maple View in your reading of this book. The Resource lists the people in the sequence in which they appear in the book. People are identified by their roles in the school or community.

Leadership Action That Matters

In the chapters that follow, the Maple View case unfolds as a story of leadership that matters. The leaders—administrators, teachers, parents, and community members—of Maple View tackle challenges such as equitable opportunities and resources to learn, culturally sensitive instruction, expectations and assumptions about student performance, and willingness to learn new ways of being with students. As educators and parents work together to resolve these problems, they learn to view their individual and collective behavior through the lens of cultural proficiency. They learn to ask, "Will this decision to act result in a more culturally proficient organization?"

Each chapter offers an opportunity to learn more about the phases of development toward cultural proficiency and to consider why it is important and how you might integrate culturally proficient practices into your daily leadership practice. The elements of culturally proficient practice provide benchmarks against which you can calibrate your leadership behavior. To begin, use the scale presented in the following section to assess your openness to the work you will undertake in this book.

Invitation: Assess Your Receptivity

To read this book with purpose, we invite you to assess your receptivity to its content. The Cultural Proficiency Receptivity Scale will assist you in your own learning. Cultural proficiency is deep, personal work that one undertakes before attempting to influence the behavior of others. Chapters 2 through 5 present the tools of cultural proficiency designed to support you in self-examination of your own values and behaviors and to enable you to examine the policies and practices of your school and its subunits.

It is our belief that personal leadership evolves from the inner work experienced by effective leaders. Leader effectiveness occurs when leaders are clear with themselves and others about what they value and believe (Banks, 1999; Covey, 1989; Heifetz, 1994; Sergiovanni, 1992). In discussing the inner work of principals, Fullan (2003) states, "The principal with a moral imperative can help realize it only by developing leadership in others" (p. xv).

The Cultural Proficiency Receptivity Scale is a nonscientific instrument designed to guide you through a process of self-reflection. The concepts in this scale derive from the information you will be reading in Chapters 2 through 5. We urge you to read each of the statements and indicate your level of agreement on the 1-to-7 Likert scale. A response of 1 indicates strong disagreement, and a response of 7 indicates strong agreement. When you have finished reading the book, we encourage you to return to the scale and reassess your levels of agreement. The purpose of this scale is to introduce you to important concepts in a manner that personalizes the content of the book. The scale is not a test and is not intended for that use.

Cultural Proficiency Receptivity Scale

I believe that all children and youth learn successfully when informed and caring teachers assist them and make sufficient resources available to them.

Strongly Disagree		Agree			Strongly Agree	
1	2	3	4	5	6	7

I want to do whatever is necessary to ensure that the students for whom I am responsible are well-educated and successful learners.

Strongly Disagree		Agree			Strongly Agree	
1	2	3	4	5	6	7

I am committed to creating both an educational environment and learning experiences for our students that honor and respect who they are.

Strongly Disagree		Agree			Strongly Agree	
1	2	3	4	5	6	7

I am willing to ask myself uncomfortable questions about racism, cultural preferences, and insufficient learning conditions and resources that are obstacles to learning for many students.

Strongly Disagree		Agree			Strongly Agree	
1	2	3	4	5	6	7

I am willing to ask questions about racism, cultural preferences, and insufficient learning conditions and resources that may be uncomfortable for others in my school or district.

Strongly Disagree		Agree			Strongly Agree	
1	2	3	4	5	6	7

I believe that all students benefit from educational practices that engage them in learning about their cultural heritage and understanding their cultural background.

Strongly Disagree		Agree			Strongly Agree	
1	2	3	4	5	6	7

I believe that all students benefit from educational practices that provide them with hope, direction, and preparation for their future lives.

Strongly Disagree		Agree			Strongly Agree	
1	2	3	4	5	6	7

It is important to know how well our district serves the various cultural and ethnic communities represented in our schools, and it is also important to understand how well served they feel by the educational practices in our schools.

Strongly Disagree		Agree			Strongly Agree	
1	2	3	4	5	6	7

It is important to know how the various cultural and ethnic communities represented in our schools view me as an educational leader and to understand how well my leadership serves their expectations.

Strongly Disagree		Agree			Strongly Agree	
1	2	3	4	5	6	7

Our district and schools are successful only when all subgroups are improving academically and socially.

Strongly Disagree		Agree			Strongly Agree	
1	2	3	4	5	6	7

Cultural discomfort and disagreements are normal occurrences in a diverse society such as ours and are parts of everyday interactions.

Strongly Disagree		Agree			Strongly Agree	
1	2	3	4	5	6	7

I believe that lack of cultural understanding and historic distrust can result in cultural discomfort and disagreements.

Strongly Disagree		Agree			Strongly Agree	
1	2	3	4	5	6	7

I believe we can learn about and implement diverse and improved instructional practices that will effectively serve all our students.

Strongly Disagree		Agree			Strongly Agree	
1	2	3	4	5	6	7

I believe we can use disaggregated data to understand more precisely the achievement status of all students in our schools, and that we can use that information to identify and implement effective instructional practices for each of them.

Strongly Disagree		Agree			Strongly Agree	
1	2	3	4	5	6	7

As a leader, it is important for me to be able to communicate across cultures and to facilitate communication among diverse cultural groups.

Strongly Disagree		Agree			Strongly Agree	
1	2	3	4	5	6	7

Review your responses, compute your total score, and record it here _____. (The range of scores is from 15 to 105.)

What does your score mean? Are you highly receptive? Are you not receptive? Are you "middling"? We ask that you resist using your initial score as anything more than a baseline of information. This book will guide and support your personal journey to becoming more effective in cross-cultural situations. Accordingly, this instrument is one tool among several reflective tools in this book that you will use in the development of a personal leadership perspective for making a difference in your school community.

When you have completed the book, we invite you to return to your responses and to analyze them to support you in your journey to cultural proficiency. If you are reading about cultural proficiency for your own personal growth, reflect on your responses and be prepared to revisit them after completing the book. At that time, you will be able to assess what you have learned about yourself, about personal change, and about complex organizational change. If you are reading this book as part of a professional development activity with colleagues or as part of a university course, discuss your responses with others and explain why you responded as you did to the several items. Then, as with the focus on personal growth, you will want to revisit your responses after completing your work and reflect on your learning about personal and complex change.

Part II

The Tools of
Cultural Proficiency

2

What Does Cultural Proficiency Look Like in Practice?

The Guiding Principles

When we teach, write about, and model the exercise of leadership, we inevitably support or challenge people's conceptions of themselves, their roles, and most importantly their ideas about how social systems make progress on problems. Leadership is a normative concept because implicit in people's notions of leadership are images of a social contract. Imagine the differences in behavior when people operate with the idea that "leadership means influencing the community to follow the leader's vision" versus "leadership means influencing the community to face its problems." . . . Leaders mobilize people to face problems, and communities make progress on problems because leaders challenge and help them to do so.

—Ronald Heifetz (1994, pp. 14–15)

Barbara Campbell: The Making of a Culturally Proficient Leader

During the 25 years that Dr. Barbara Campbell has been professionally involved in public education, she has become increasingly more aware of the cultural obstacles students face in schools and classrooms and the effects those obstacles have on student learning and achievement. As a young African American woman, she had learned to manage transitions among the sociocultural borders and barriers that she encountered, but that managing process required her to live with her family in one cultural world and go to school in another. Thinking about it now, she can still feel the anxiety and stress that she experienced as a student—and even as a young teacher.

Taking a few last sips of coffee at the small, round table in her kitchen, Barbara reviews her notes for the principals' meeting later this morning. It would be so simple if she could just mandate cultural competence in every school. She sits back in her chair and smiles slightly, knowing that such a mandate is impossible. She also knows that people will look at her behavior as an example of the changes she wants them to make in their own behavior. She has thought about this meeting for so long—and now, in just a few hours, she will be sitting with the principals and preparing them to embark on a journey toward cultural competence with the teachers in their schools. Glancing at the clock, she sees it is time to go.

Later, in the conference room, Dr. Campbell asks the principals to reflect on a simple but important question: "Whose needs does your school best serve?"

"Students," says Sam Brewer, the recently appointed principal of Pine Hills High School.

Barbara smiles and responds enthusiastically, "Great!" She then asks Sam and the other principals in the group to consider which group or groups of students are most successful and why:

> I don't want an answer right now. I want you to meet with your school's leadership team and review your students' achievement results. Look at every subgroup and determine who is doing well and who is not succeeding. And then ask yourselves two questions: "Why are we getting these results?" and "Are these the results we want?"

Standing up, Barbara distributes each school's achievement reports. Pointing out that the results are disaggregated by student subgroups, Barbara says,

It's very important to understand the dynamics in your schools that are producing the results you're getting. Go back and study these results with your teams. Then study your schools. What are your expectations for each subgroup? Are you meeting those expectations? Why?

Sitting down again, Barbara lowers her voice,

When we meet again in 2 weeks, I want each of you to be prepared to describe the obstacles that seem to be getting in the way of student achievement in each subgroup. I also want you to be ready to discuss how the norms for expected behavior, the structures—like scheduling and grouping, the patterns of activity, and the rules and procedures in the school—may be contributing to the obstacles your students are experiencing.

Barbara hands each principal a set of data collection worksheets:

This packet will guide your work with your teams. You'll see that I'm asking you to think about the dynamics of your schools in relation to the five principles of cultural proficiency that support our district mission. Oh, and one other very important thing, I want you to work with your teams to identify five strong values that make your school the school it is.

Barbara stands up:

I'll see you in 2 weeks. Call me if any questions come up. I'm looking forward to our next meeting. And, thanks for being on time today. It shows respect for everyone's time and for our time together as a group. I really appreciate that.

■ Reflective Activity

Consider the questions that the superintendent, Dr. Campbell, asked the principals in her district: Which groups of students are best served by your school? Which students are not well served? Why are we getting these results?

- As you reflect on your own district, school, classroom, or program, how would you respond to these important questions?

- How is your own leadership informed by your response?

_____

_____

_____

_____

_____

_____

Mobilizing Communities to Make Progress—Without Easy Answers

A culturally proficient leader influences others to make changes in their values, beliefs, and attitudes. Challenging and supporting others to build their capacity to confront difficult sociocultural problems in their community and to take them on successfully is a priority for a leader intent on fostering culturally proficient behavior among others. Indeed, such a leader makes it his or her purpose to help the community become culturally competent and to support it in building productive, functional patterns of social interaction.

In our work with schools and districts, we often find that mission, vision, and core value statements often satisfy some external requirements rather than guide and give purpose to the real work of the school or district. As an alternative to such practice, leaders can choose to offer authentic benchmarks of progress by charting a course using the five principles of cultural proficiency. To use them effectively in this way requires understanding the five principles at a deep level and embracing them as core leadership values. The five principles are as follows:

- Culture is a predominant force in people's lives.
- The dominant culture serves people in varying degrees.
- People have both personal identities and group identities.
- Diversity within cultures is vast and significant.
- Each individual and each group has unique cultural values and needs.

The Guiding Principles of Culturally Proficient Leadership

More often than not, when educators talk about school change, they are describing modifications in the structures, patterns, and processes of education practice. Structural changes such as adopting new scheduling patterns or new grouping procedures, or even requiring new curriculum materials, do have the potential to reform instructional practices and thereby improve student learning for some students. However, structural changes alone are insufficient to produce the kinds of deep conversions that have the potential to transform the social and cultural conditions within a school or district. The five principles of cultural proficiency offer a guided pathway for school leaders as they shift their perspectives on school change from reforming structures, policies, and rules in schools to transforming relationships, interactions, and behaviors of the people within schools. Holders of the school reform perspective concentrate their efforts on how to change structures and policies. The school reform perspective too often flows from a predictable mission statement that espouses goals that are not reflective of the authentic day-to-day practices of people in the school. A commonplace mission statement purports that all students can achieve at a high level; however, in practice this espoused goal ignores the fact that many students from identifiable demographic groups do not succeed. In not having an authentic mission statement, schools with a reform perspective resort to default mission statements with a core belief that some children and youth cannot or will not learn. Reeves (2000) notes that this unstated belief is expressed in code words, such as "diversity" and "demographics." In a school with a reform perspective, one might hear, "We're not doing too badly, given our diversity" (or demographics).

Conversely, the school leader who holds a transformational perspective focuses on leadership and school practices to meet the generative opportunities and needs of diverse communities. Leaders engaged in transformational activities build on the experiences of their students, and they direct their own leadership activities in ways that involve all members of the school or district community in becoming culturally proficient and able to meet the challenging problems they encounter together.

The guiding principles open up opportunities to build culturally proficient and functionally diverse educational communities in which people interact with one another in respectful and culturally responsive ways.

■ Principle 1: Culture Is a Predominant Force

Nuri Robins, Lindsey, Lindsey, and Terrell (2002) state that you cannot *not* have a culture. You are your culture, you live your culture, and you express your culture whether you intend to or not. Your culture is a defining aspect of your humanity. As a school leader, it is important to acknowledge culture as a predominant force in shaping behaviors, values, and attitudes in schools. Culture determines how you interact with your teachers, staff, students, and members of the community and how they interact with you and one another. Culture determines how individuals react to things that happen in the school or district and the community it serves. The organizational norms, the school climate, and the unwritten rules of your organization are all reflections of the culture. Culture is more than just one characteristic, such as race or ethnicity; culture is about being part of a group. Culture reflects the unique defining blend of features among individuals within groups and includes variables such as socioeconomic status, profession or trade, academic preparation, experience, gender, language, education, sexual orientation, psychological state, and political views. Culture is the mix of beliefs and behaviors of any group that distinguish them as a group and make them who they are. As individuals, we belong to many different cultural groups, depending on our relationships and interactions with others.

Culture can have both positive and negative implications. One who is aware of his or her culture can use that knowledge in ways that promote inclusiveness or exclusiveness. A negative aspect of culture, cultural bias, generally involves preferential interaction with others who are like us. Bias may stimulate disdain for or fear of those who are not like us. Cultural differences—without cultural understanding or sensitivity—may provoke disapproval or even contempt. Lack of cultural knowledge or experience may stimulate anger, fear, guilt, or even hate between different groups.

Consider the following examples of culture in everyday school activities. In the brief incidents that follow, we return to Maple View School District to examine the dynamics of culture at work in schools. Each incident represents a composite of actual events and authentic conversations that we have observed during our work with prekindergarten through Grade 12 schools. Keep in mind that these are conversations of educators engaged in the challenging work of personal transformation.

*Conversation 1: What Is
Important at Pine Hills High?*

The school leadership team at Pine Hills High School has been working this year with a school improvement coach, Dr. Charles Banks, to look carefully at their student performance results and determine why there is such uneven achievement across subgroups of students. Disaggregated reports reveal that students who come to the school from the east side neighborhoods of Maple View are achieving at much lower levels than are students from the more affluent west side neighborhoods. Dr. Banks, or Charles, as the team calls him, has been helping the team look at how the school's dominant cultural identity may be contributing to the school's achievement "problem." Charles has given the team members Polaroid cameras and asked them to look around at the cultural artifacts in the school, take pictures of them, and bring the pictures back for examination and discussion. He has suggested that they look for such things as posted signs, announcements, and directions; displays of student work; and awards and other clues about the cultural identity of the school.

Forty-five minutes later, the team members are back with their pictures and already in conversations regarding what the pictures reveal about the school. Two teachers, Rob Moore and Joel Peters, are looking closely at a set of pictures. Sam Brewer, the principal at Pine Hills, joins them, and the discussion unfolds:

Joel: This is pretty interesting. It seems like 75% of these pictures have something to do with sports.

Rob   Well, I guess sports rule at Pine Hills, and that explains
(laughingly):   why the athletes get preferential treatment and special privileges.

Joel   And we thought this was going to be difficult.
(smirking):

Sam: At the risk of sounding defensive, I'm assuming—no, hoping—you're just teasing. Even if the pictures don't show it, our emphasis on accountability is clear and surely points out that we've moved way beyond that old stereotype of jock school to a school that values achievement.

Rob (more seriously):	No, I was serious, even though I said it somewhat in jest. Just look at these pictures. Combine that with the amount of time student athletes are out of class. Or, just walk in the front door of the school and take notice of what is in our display cabinets.
Sam:	Do you have any idea how many students stay in school solely because of sports and that 40% of our students participate in extracurricular activities?
Joel:	Wait a minute, guys. It seems to me that you two are in agreement about the culture of the school. The difference, if there is one, is the way each of you is interpreting the data we have. Is the perception of athletics as "all important" either positive or negative? As a point of agreement, you both point out the centrality of athletics at this school. What else is important, and how do we show it?

Joel was particularly insightful in recognizing that both Bob and Sam saw athletics as a dynamic shaping the attitudes, values, benefits, and behavior of the school. Moreover, the pictures revealed that the school's identity was steeped in a culture of competitive athletics. The trophy case in the school lobby and the preferential treatment of athletes are but two artifacts that convey this message.

■ Reflective Activity

Consider Joel's question, "What else is important, and how do we show it?" How could the Pine Hills faculty and students demonstrate that other activities are important at Pine Hills? Describe the behaviors and artifacts we might see at the school.

_____

_____

_____

_____

_____

_____

Conversation 2: Why Can't They Just Be Like Us?

The second conversation involves an informal exchange among Connie Barkely, a third-grade teacher; Joan Stephens, a fifth-grade teacher; and Rose Diaz-Harris, the assistant principal at Maple View Elementary School. The school is experiencing a change in the student population due to a large influx of immigrants from Central America. Rose and the two teachers have gathered around the coffeepot in the lunchroom and are serving themselves before the start of the weekly staff meeting. This will be the final meeting before the annual 2-week winter break:

Connie (yawning as she pours her coffee):	Wow! Am I ready for this Christmas vacation or what? You know, having so many children absent this week is so annoying. I know I'll have to help them catch up when they get back in January.
Joan (cradling her warm cup in both hands):	I can't imagine what the parents are thinking. It's just not fair. Parents should know better than to uproot their kids and whisk them off for an extra-long break. They must know this is not in the kids' best interest. What's wrong with these parents? Don't they know their kids are going to fall behind?
Connie:	I'm so glad you said that. My grandparents were immigrants, and when they came here, they decided to become Americans. They made their children speak English, and you certainly didn't see them going back to the old country every chance they got!
Joan (laughing):	I know! I know! My father's grandparents came here from Ireland. They used to joke about leaving the old sod behind them. They couldn't afford to go back, and they certainly wouldn't have yanked their kids out of school to do it. They were so grateful their kids were getting a free education.
Rose (filling a coffee filter and making a fresh pot of coffee):	Whoa! Whoa! Ladies, aren't we jumping to a lot of hasty conclusions here? The parents don't know what is best for their children? Uprooting their own children? The experience of European and Caribbean immigrants 50 years ago being the same as those of Central American immigrants today? Perhaps we are using our own assumptions and experiences to denigrate others. Have you taken the time to talk with the parents about this?

Rose, the assistant principal, has rightly intervened in a conversation that evidenced the bias and judgment that often accompany a lack of cultural knowledge and understanding about actions that are different from those with which we are comfortable. Both conversations illustrate the influence of culture in our everyday lives.

■ Reflective Activity

Consider Rose's question, "Have you taken the time to talk with the parents about this?" In Rose's position, how might you coach Connie and Joan to become more culturally knowledgeable and understanding of actions that differ from their own personal experiences?

_____

_____

_____

_____

_____

_____

■ Principle 2: People Are Served in Varying Degrees by the Dominant Culture

As a member of the dominant culture, you may not notice the many ways in which the culture of your district, school, or group impacts those who do not know or are not benefiting from the cultural norms or privileges. What works in favor of you in your school, your district, and your community may work against members of other cultural groups. Often, when members of dominant cultures recognize that cultural differences exist, they suggest that the person in the non-dominant culture simply learn a new way of doing things: Become an American! In such a case, the word *American* is synonymous with "a person who accepts assimilation into the dominant culture." When considered in this context, the person who assimilates into the dominant culture initially accepts a subordinate relationship with the dominant culture. Suarez-Orozco (1985) describes this phenomenon based on a study of 200 Central American immigrant students. The students and their parents held a dual frame of reference in which they compared their experiences in the United States with their situations in their home countries. The students who succeeded academically believed that the nature of opportunity in this country was better, fairer, and more accessible to them than in their home countries. Despite facing and dealing with difficult and challenging conditions in this country, they persevered by holding to a folk theory of "making it" and to a perspective that no matter how hard conditions were in the United States, they were not as bad as at "home."

This solution burdens members of the nondominant group to adopt—or at the very least espouse the adoption of—the dominant culture's values. Alternatively, a culturally proficient solution would seek a commitment to a dynamic relationship in which all parties learn from each other and adapt as they adjust to their differences.

In reading the following two illustrations, pay particular attention to how cultural differences are recognized, embraced, or both. The first conversation takes place at Pine Hills High School, which has been experiencing profound demographic shifts in its student population. The second incident is from Maple View Elementary School, which has decided to build its language development program based on the cultural experiences of the students.

Conversation 3: Traditions Are Strong: We Are Who We Were

Twelve years ago, Maple View High School had a stable, white, middle-class population. Most of the parents were either professionals or "stay-at-home" moms. The school had a typical college prep curriculum that appeared to serve the needs of most of the students and their parents. During the past 6 years, the community has been transformed by the immigration of people from Central America, Russia, and the Middle East. In addition, the school has grown from a population of 1,200 to more than 1,500 students, which has created stressful conditions such as larger classes and overcrowding in the hallways and cafeteria. Additional teachers have been hired to accommodate the growing student population. Many of the new teachers are specialists in teaching English as a second language. In effect, Maple View has two separate faculties—teachers who taught at the school before "the change" and those who have come to the school as a result of the demographic transition. The core curriculum and instructional practices of veteran teachers have changed very little throughout the transition. After several frustrating years of dealing ineffectively with conditions of overcrowding, declining test scores, and general dissatisfaction with the school's results, the district contracted with a school improvement coach. The coach, Dr. Stephanie Barnes, was to work with the school's principal, Oscar Medina, and his faculty to help them devise ways in which the school can be more successful for all its students.

During the next several months, Dr. Barnes, along with some of her graduate students, conducted interviews with every constituent group–administrators, teachers, classified staff, students, parents, and other members of the local community. They interviewed virtually every staff member. They observed and recorded instruction in classrooms across the campus and attended meetings of various leadership groups on campus, including administrative, departmental, parent, and student groups. In addition, Dr. Barnes asked all the constituent groups to complete surveys. As a result of their inquiry, Dr. Barnes and her students discovered that the data revealed some important findings about what was going on in the school. In fact, the process was inundated by data. The irrefutable facts confirmed that standardized test scores continued to decline, there was ethnic unrest among the three immigrant groups, and the educators were frustrated with their perceived ineffectiveness. Dr. Barnes met with all the teachers and administrators in a minimum-day staff meeting in which she planned to discuss her findings and solicit feedback from the staff. The following was part of the discussion:

Dr. Barnes (referring to a Power Point slide):	So, you can see from this summary on these slides, the data are pretty clear on several points: First, Maple View High has experienced a great shift in demographics over the past 6 years: from a student population of more than 63% white middle class to a population of more than 50% students of color and students who are learning English. Second, the school's population has increased by 25% in that same period of time, and you have accommodated that growth by adding portables and new teachers. Third, standardized test scores have declined, and, related to that, the curriculum has remained relatively unchanged over the years. Fourth, most of the instruction I have witnessed over these months can be best described as teacher centered. Fifth, ethnic tensions among students appear to be confined mostly to the on-campus commons areas, and there appears to be very little evidence of this tension within the classrooms.

Jack Thompson (a science teacher):	Dr. Barnes, in that third finding, are you suggesting that we, the teachers, are the problem? If so, I'm offended!
Janice Thompson (the school's counselor):	Me, too! I've been at this school for 15 years, and I've experienced firsthand all that you are describing. You couldn't ask for a more hardworking, dedicated group of teachers or administrators.
Maxine Parks (an English teacher):	I'm on the steering committee that has been working with Stephanie, and I don't think that's what she's trying to say or imply. You know, Dr. Barnes, this is the third time I've seen your findings, and one thing occurs to me for the first time. I, too, have been on this faculty for this entire transition of our community. My question for all of us to consider is: Are we are still trying to teach the students who used to go to school here?

The staff and Dr. Barnes were silent. Maxine's question was stunning. Had she identified the crux of the situation? Was this a case in which indifference to cultural diversity had resulted in obstacles to student learning? It seemed so obvious, and yet no one had seen it.

■ Reflective Activity

Consider Maxine's question, "Are we are still trying to teach the students who used to go to school here?" How might you coach the Maple View High staff to recognize and acknowledge that their indifference and inattention to cultural diversity and differing cultural values may be an obstacle to providing responsive instructional approaches that would be consciously designed to meet varying student needs?

_____

_____

_____

_____

_____

Conversation 4: Who Is Being Served?

In this conversation, Ed Johnson, the principal of Maple View Elementary School, is working with Janice Ross, a principal of an elementary school in a neighboring district. Janice is meeting with Ed at his school, and she is helping him analyze some student performance data. They are colleagues in a doctoral program in a nearby city. As part of his dissertation, Ed wants to develop an experimental reading program specifically targeted to meet the educational and social needs of the African American boys in his school. Janice wants to design a similar program for the students at her school. Together, they have been reviewing research on innovations in teaching reading and have also been studying the results of reading programs that have been producing successful results with African American boys. Both schools are part of a statewide accountability process in which they are targeting growth in reading for each grade level and for each demographic subgroup at the school:

Ed: Janice, I really appreciate your help with this data. It's so helpful to have someone to bounce ideas off of.

Janice: Well, you've already helped me so much with my data. I wouldn't be as far along if I didn't have your help.

Ed: As you can see, this group of boys are among the lowest readers in our district. That has to change! I've talked with Dr. Campbell, our superintendent, and she is very supportive and has given me a lot of latitude to do what research suggests is effective. She also has offered to give me some funding to support this work.

Janice: So, Ed, what do you really want to accomplish?

Ed: Well, like everyone else, I want these kids to be good readers.

Janice: And . . . what will that look like? What will be your indicators of success?

Ed: The research findings you and I have been studying provide some ideas about specific reading approaches for African American males, but . . .

Janice: Hmmmm. I hear a tone of hesitancy in your voice. What's that about?

Ed: Well, there is a language and reading skills development program available from the university. Several large city districts have tried it. It emphasizes the connection between reading and writing and helps kids understand the differences between spoken and written English. It has a track record of success with African American kids, especially boys.

Janice: And?

Ed: Well, I'm afraid that many of our teachers, and maybe even some members of the community, will react negatively to it because it doesn't fit traditional models for teaching reading. It has such a specific focus.

Janice: Wait a minute, Ed. I'm confused. Are you talking about what is best for your students, or whether or not the adults will accept it? Which is more important to you?

Ed: Wow, how could I miss that one? I've been so concerned about how people might react to this program and how I'd have to build a case for it. I've completely sidestepped what these kids deserve. Man, I can't believe I'm even saying this. I was ready to put the adults' needs ahead of the unique needs of our students!

Ed sat back in his chair, shaking his head. He felt embarrassed because he had truly lost track of what was important. Indeed, he had been willing to set aside his true purpose. Although he felt chagrined, he also was grateful to Janice for helping him recognize and acknowledge his actions.

■ Reflective Activity

Think about Ed's statement, "I was ready to put the adult's needs ahead of the unique needs of our students!" How might you coach Ed to be conscious of the cultural values—both his own and those of others—that may be obstacles to providing appropriate and responsive instructional approaches that are specifically designed to meet varying student needs?

_____

_____

_____

_____

_____

_____

In each of these conversations, the working assumptions were that the nondominant groups need to conform to what is acceptable, traditional, and comfortable for the dominant group. In the first situation, it was the immigrant students, and in the second it was the African American boys. The educators portrayed in these conversations were not intentionally trying to harm students. However, in each case they were operating from the underlying, unexamined assumptions that the nondominant group must conform to the expectation of the dominant group. The question we must consider in each case is, "At what cost is this expectation realized?"

■ Principle 3: Acknowledge the Group Identity of Individuals

Although it is important to treat all people as individuals, it is also important to acknowledge the group identity of individuals. The dignity of a person is not guaranteed unless the dignity of his or her group is also preserved. It is important to remember that most people have one or two groups with which they identify strongly. Making negative comments or reinforcing a negative stereotype about the group is insulting to its members. Moreover, attempting to separate people from their group by telling them, "You're different; you're not like those other _____s," is offensive and denies that the person may identify strongly with other _____s.

Garcia (1999) draws on anthropological research as he examines the educational implications of the "group-oriented concept of culture." He explains that the goal of instruction is the education of the individual and expands on this by stating,

> The relevance of this problem lies in the possible consequences of the group-oriented concept of culture for the perceptions and expectations of teachers in their interactions with culturally diverse children. A group-oriented concept may serve to distract the teacher's attention from the student's particular experience of culture-generating processes, in and outside of school. The culture concept adopted by the teacher greatly affects teacher-student interaction. The assumptions a teacher makes about the student's culture, whether right or wrong, may stereotype the student and thus preclude the flexible, realistic, and open-minded teacher-student interaction needed for effective instruction. The effect of this stereotyping on students is significant, since the educational process is fundamentally a process of social interaction, with socialization as a primary goal. (p. 69)

Each individual assembles his or her version of the larger culture with which he or she identifies. Garcia (1999) builds on this idea and suggests that any culture is a distributive phenomenon in that its elements and constructs are varyingly distributed among individual members of the group. Each group member constructs the identifying cultural variables in ways that are different from other members. Garcia quotes Schwartz (1978), who argues that the sharing and nonsharing of cultural constructs among members of a group are both fundamentally essential to a society's viability. Schwartz (1978) further argues that "diversity increases a society's cultural inventory, whereas what any individual could contain within his or her head would make up a very small culture pool. Commonality then permits communication and coordination in social life" (as quoted in Garcia, 1999, p. 438).

This view helps us to address the issues of cultural diversity in schools. Within the framework of a larger, shared culture, we can recognize simultaneously a student's membership in a cultural group and those characteristics that define the student as a unique individual.

The two conversations that follow address the educational issues related to the ways in which teachers recognize and respond to their students. When teachers hold a view of a student sharing characteristics of a cultural group that he or she does not share with others outside the group, while also viewing the student as an individual with an idiosyncratic expression of those cultural characteristics, they position themselves to deal with both the individual and the culture. How teachers respond to students from culturally diverse populations influences what students learn and how they learn it. Teachers should be well prepared to instruct students in various content areas, and they must be sensitive to the ways in which a student's culture impacts what and how he or she learns. The first incident is from Pine Hills High School and relates to the faculty's decision to acknowledge the group identities of gay and lesbian students. The second situation illustrates an interaction between a consultant and the teachers at Maple View Middle School as they learn to recognize students' group identities.

Conversation 5: The Individual Emerges From the Group

The leadership committee at Pine Hills High School has become increasingly aware of an emerging issue rising from gay and lesbian students sharing their sexual orientation identities in classroom discussions and during cocurricular club meetings. For most of the students at the school, it is a relative nonissue; however, a small group of male students has begun to harass the gay and lesbian students. Last week, one of the students was beaten severely after a football game.

Sam Brewer, the principal at Pine Hills, convened the leadership committee on Monday afternoon following the assault. The following conversation took place at the meeting:

Sam Brewer:	We simply can't tolerate this kind of behavior on this campus. It's up to us around this table to make sure the violence stops!
Jim Jones (physical education teacher and football coach):	I couldn't agree more. Maybe we need to get these students some counseling to help them cope with their sexual preference or choice, or whatever the problem is.
Alice Falls (history teacher):	Jim, the term is *sexual orientation.* Your sexual orientation is to heterosexuality. The students who are the victims in this assault were attacked because they have a homosexual orientation. I know that some folks try to make this a moral issue or a mental health issue. You suggested these students need counseling.
Jim:	Well, I wanted to get them some help. They've been threatened and hurt. Some counseling might help.
Alice:	Counseling in order to become "normal"? Their problem isn't that they're not normal; they have a different sexual orientation. They're different from you and me, that's all. What they need most is fairness from all of us.
Sam:	Intolerance and misunderstanding historically have been used against any group that is "different" from the mainstream, from what the majority or dominant group thinks is acceptable or normal.
Jim:	I think I'm beginning to see what you guys are talking about.
Alice:	Look at our history. Women couldn't vote or own property or do certain jobs because they weren't

men. Black folks couldn't be free, couldn't vote because they weren't white. The dominant group uses its power to say what's okay and what isn't okay.

Sam: For us, right now, right here at Pine Hills High School, the issue is that we're responsible for educating all of our students well. If we're going to teach our gay and lesbian students effectively, we must acknowledge them for who they are. We also must remember that in addition to being gay or lesbian, they're still individual Pine Hills students—math students, history students, athletes, school leaders, and the children of folks in this community.

Jim: You know, I hope I don't come across as a thoughtless person, but you guys are raising things I've never even thought about. I mean, I guess I knew this stuff at some level, but I feel like I'm on information overload. You know, right now I just need to think about this. I haven't thought about it this way. You've opened my eyes; thanks for helping me see this. Man, I feel really awkward.

Jim is shifting his perspective as a result of a conversation with his colleagues. What was it about the conversation that helped him become more aware of his assumptions?

■ Reflective Activity

Consider the way this conversation influenced Jim and helped him to rethink his assumptions about a group of students. Now that his awareness of this issue is heightened, how can Jim learn to recognize and acknowledge the identity of gay and lesbian students while accepting and respecting them as individuals?

_____

_____

_____

_____

_____

_____

Conversation 6: Whom Did You Expect to See?

One of Dr. Barbara Campbell's main goals for the Maple View School District has been to work toward a more culturally proficient organization. She has involved the district's teachers in many professional development sessions focusing on cultural diversity and proficiency. Most of the training has taken place at the individual school sites to encourage team building and to shape school cultures in which the people in them share the goal of becoming more culturally responsive and proficient in interacting with diverse populations. The staff at Maple View Middle School has been working with Dr. Jesse Phillips, a well-known author and educator, to understand the implications of students' attitudes toward members of the group whose language they are learning. Dr. Phillips, or "Jesse," as he likes to be called, has facilitated a lively session that focused on research suggesting that students' positive attitudes toward the culture of the target language correspond to higher language proficiency in that language. The session has just ended, and Jesse is gathering his materials and charts and organizing them to carry out to his car. While he is involved in packing up, Bob Moore, a sixth-grade social studies teacher, approaches Jesse with a question:

Bob:	Did I understand you to say you're an American Indian?
Jesse:	Well . . . yes. Actually, I said I was of Native American heritage.
Bob:	I don't mean to be rude, but you don't look like a Native American. I mean, I've visited several reservations in the Southwest, and you just don't look like anyone I have ever seen there.
Jesse (laughing):	Is it the light brown hair and green eyes that are confusing you?
Bob (nodding in agreement):	Yeah, that's what it is. I mean, you could even be one of my neighbors.
Jesse:	Hmmm. Sounds like that raises a concern.
Bob:	Well, yeah, I guess it could be a problem.
Jesse:	Were you thinking that you might tell me a joke or make some comment about Indians and not know who I am? You're afraid you might be embarrassed?

Bob (looking at the floor):	Well, yeah, I guess that's it.
Jesse:	What does that suggest to you?
Bob:	Well, during the session today, you said something like, "Insulting one member of a group, insults all members of that group."
Jesse:	That's right.
Bob:	I guess that has personal meaning for me now. When I came up here to talk with you just now, I didn't expect our conversation to lead to this topic. I learned something important just now. Thanks.
Jesse (smiling):	Well, Bob, you're welcome. Just promise me that you'll take this learning with you as you work with your colleagues, your students, and members of this community. And please remember, it takes more courage to speak up for people in their absence than it does in their presence. In this case, the difference appeared to be invisible.

In each of these conversations, assumptions about cultural groups and, by extension, the individuals who are members of the group led to misunderstanding about both. Conscious tolerance, acceptance, and openness to diversity enable us to interact effectively with individuals and groups who are different from us.

■ Reflective Activity

Consider the way this conversation influenced Bob and helped him to become conscious of his assumptions and question them. Now that he is more aware of how his assumptions influence his actions, how can Bob use this new learning to help himself interact more effectively with culturally diverse individuals and groups?

_____

_____

_____

_____

_____

_____

■ Principle 4: Recognize Diversity Within Cultures

Recognizing the inevitable diversity within cultures is just as important as acknowledging the differences that exist between diverse cultures. Individuals exist as unique members of cultural groups that include many variations. Likewise, cultural groups exist as distinctive collections of idiosyncratic members, creating complexity within groups. Consider this example: European Americans as a cultural group share some common characteristics but vary widely in cultural characteristics such as social customs, linguistic heritage, economic status, religious affiliations, and educational opportunities. The same statement would hold true for African Americans. Indeed, we learn from sociological studies (Gordon, 1964; Myrdal, 1944) that upper- and middle-class African Americans share more cultural characteristics with upper- and middle-class European Americans than they do with lower-class African Americans and European Americans. Every cultural or ethnic group in the United States can be disaggregated along socioeconomic boundaries. The members of each socioeconomic group (e.g., wealthy Americans, middle-class Americans, and Americans living below the poverty line) share more characteristics with other members of their socioeconomic status group than they do with the racial or ethnic groups to which they also belong. Nonetheless, cultural mythologies grow abundantly in the United States. Assumptions, fed by lack of experience, fear of the unknown, social distance, and misinformation, often lead to monolithic perceptions, stereotypes, and prejudices between and among cultural groups. These cultural mythologies are neither neutral nor inconsequential. They are obstacles to progress to accepting cultural differences and to effective interactions among people who are members of diverse cultural groups.

Culturally proficient exchanges require people to embrace difference as a positive attribute rather than a detracting and negative feature. By acknowledging and valuing both inter- and intracultural differences, educational leaders can provide their faculties, staffs, students, and parents with access to information about people who are unlike themselves in various ways but who also share some common characteristics and similarities. Through such efforts, leaders can create the possibility of educational environments that foster trust, safety, and enhancement of self for the people who work and learn in them.

The conversations that follow are illustrations of organizational and individual acknowledgment and valuing of diversity within cultures. In the first interaction, the principal is working with grade-level teams to develop more effective approaches to the math curriculum. The second conversation takes place in an arts magnet middle school.

Conversation 7: Each Culture Is Unique

Laura Alvarez is beginning her second year as the assistant principal of Maple View Elementary School. This year, she and her staff have made a commitment to increase their students' math and reading literacy. Working with the district's math and language arts specialists, Laura has helped her staff recognize some of the unique educational needs of the diverse subgroup populations among their students. Maple View Elementary has three distinct subgroups: newly arrived immigrants from Mexico who are primarily English language learners, second-generation Mexican American students whose families are struggling financially, and African American students who live in public housing and whose families are also struggling financially. Laura and the teachers at Maple View understand that each subgroup of students has specific learning needs and will benefit from instructional strategies that are designed to build on their individual strengths while responding to their specific needs as a group. Laura also knows that each of her grade level teams has its own culture and particular way of interacting with one another. Listen to her conversation with the district's math specialist, Dr. Belinda Jackson, as they plan a professional development program for the year:

Belinda: Laura, I'm so excited about this new math adoption program, and I'm really interested to know how you are planning to help the staff with implementation.

Laura: Well, thanks to you, the district is providing us with two professional development days in August for the publishing company representatives to begin the training. We have all the materials on campus already, so I'm thinking that their training will be just a general orientation. While all of this good, I'm feeling uneasy and I'm not sure why.

Belinda: Okay, Laura, talk to me about "being uneasy." What's that all about?

Laura: Oh Belinda, it's just that, well, candidly, some of our teams are ready to go and others are not.

Belinda: It's just like one of your favorite phrases, "We're talking about the elephant in the middle of the room that no one can see."

Laura: Belinda, what are you talking about? What does that mean?

Belinda: Laura, we've talked about this before. You've told me that it's no secret, each grade level team has its own culture.

Laura: You're absolutely right, Belinda! It doesn't matter what I give the second-grade team, they're going to take it and run with it. At the other end of the continuum is the fifth-grade team. They can hardly stand to be in the same room at the same time. Developing collaborative relationships among them is going to take a very specific strategy.

Belinda: So, okay, now we know what we've got to do. Let's get to work.

Laura   Yes, we sure do! Coaching is going to be different from
(sighing): team to team. Thanks, Belinda! You're always such a great help to me. What would I do without you?

Laura and Belinda have acknowledged the different cultures that exist among the grade level teams, and now they are better prepared to meet the needs of students through meeting the diverse needs of each team.

■ Reflective Activity

Consider the way this conversation influenced Laura and helped give her the direction she needed to meet the differing professional development needs of her grade level groups. Now that she recognizes the differences and understands why they exist, how should she move forward with her planning?

_____

_____

_____

_____

_____

_____

The next conversation provides us with insight as to how differences within racial or ethnic cultural groups might be manifested.

Conversation 8: Each Individual Is Unique

The Maple View Arts Magnet School is a small district kindergarten through Grade 8 (K–8) charter school supported by a group of parents who want to develop educational opportunities in the visual and performing arts for their own and other children in the district. The mission of the school is to foster each student's individual talents in the arts and to support his or her overall academic success. Students who graduate from the K–8 program are able to go directly into the district's arts magnet high school.

Ella Chapman is an African American parent of two students enrolled in Maple View Arts. Her son, Jeffrey, is a seventh grader, and her daughter, Cheryl, is in the fourth grade. Both children are musically gifted and often perform with the local musical theater group. Ella and her husband, Gregory, are also talented professional musicians who met while they were students at the Juilliard School of Music in New York City. They both perform professionally in the regional symphony orchestra.

Anh Me Vu is a Vietnamese parent whose daughter, Melanie, is a member of the school's corps de ballet. Melanie Vu is in the sixth grade, and her brother Jason is a third-grader. Melanie is an accomplished musician and a talented dancer. Jason is showing skill as a young violinist. Anh Me, a gifted musician herself, also attended Juilliard and performs regularly with the regional symphony orchestra.

Let's listen to this conversation between the two parents following a recital at the school:

Ella Chapman (welcoming and smiling):	Anh Me, it's so good to see you. Your Melanie is such a beautiful dancer. Is she considering joining a professional ballet company's school?
Anh Me Vu:	Oh, Ella, it's good to see you, too. Our rehearsals last week with the symphony were pretty grueling, weren't they? I've been recovering over the weekend.
Ella:	That was quite a workout all right.
Anh Me:	Ella, thanks for the generous praise for Melanie. She works very hard at developing her dancing, and she loves it. I'm not sure she's ready to commit to it as a career. We'll just have to wait and see. And Ella, you

	must be very proud of Jeffrey. I understand that he placed first in the regional violin competition last week. I hope our son, Jason, will someday play as well as your Jeffrey does.
Ella:	Yes, we're so very proud of Jeffrey. Musical talent seems to run in our family. Our family, like yours, has had three generations attend Julliard. Jeffrey will be the fourth generation.
Anh Me:	Wow, I'm surprised you knew I attended Julliard, too! Most people who look at me and my family think we just arrived from Vietnam and can't speak English.
Ella (smiling and nodding):	I do understand that frustration, believe me. I've lived with it my entire life.
Anh Me (laughing):	You know, when Melanie first applied to attend the arts magnet, one of the panelists asked her if her family was one of "the boat people." Melanie didn't know what the woman was talking about. That didn't stop this woman; she went on and said she was so surprised that Melanie spoke English so clearly. Melanie didn't know what to make of it, and I was totally exasperated. I went up to her after the interview and told her that in addition to English, every member of our family is also fluent in Vietnamese and French! I'm not sure I had any impact on her stereotypes. I'm afraid that's just the way she sees the world.
Ella:	Listen, Anh Me, I can relate to that! You did the right thing in calling her on her stereotyping. I know it's sometimes hard to do, but we can't just accept that kind of thoughtlessness. I'll admit that it's happening less and less often, but our family sometimes still experiences that same kind of insensitivity. It gets so old, but we've got to stay on top of it and educate others when it happens.

This conversation illustrates the experiences of two individuals stunned by thoughtless, insensitive stereotyping. The cultural group that individuals are part of may be organizational, economic, educational, racial, or occupational. Regardless, there is always tremendous individual diversity and variation within the group. Individual differences among the members of a group are as important to the development of a person's self-image and identity as is membership within that group. Educators have the unique opportunity to continue to learn about the members of the communities they serve, both as members of their cultural communities and as the individuals they are.

■ Reflective Activity

Consider the way this conversation helped the two parents, Ella and Anh Me, understand and appreciate more fully each other's unique characteristics and background. How can they put this new learning to use in countering and diminishing thoughtless and insensitive stereotyping of themselves and their families and also other unique members of their cultural groups?

_____

_____

_____

_____

_____

_____

■ Principle 5: Respect Unique Cultural Needs

Research about how people develop cultural identities suggests that very young children in preschool are aware of differences among cultural and ethnic groups (Ogbu, 1992). After this awareness develops, children begin forming attitudes about their own and other cultural groups. Using information available to them from the adults around them and their own interactions and experiences, young children shape ethnic and cultural identities based on their perceptions of where they (and their group) rank in relation to other ethnic and cultural groups (Gollnick & Chinn, 1990). These early perceptions are deeply imprinted and influence people's ethnic and cultural identities for the rest of their lives. Garcia (1999) suggests that the cultural organization of a society, specifically the roles and status assigned to cultural groups within a society, is a major determinant of educational underachievement. Ogbu adds that social and cultural stratification leads to an individual's perception, whether negative or positive, of both his own status and the social placement of his sociocultural group within the hierarchy of the broader societal structure. In other words, from a very young age, people understand their "place" in society. Furthermore, Ogbu suggests an individual's perceived social placement directly affects his sense of individual identity, values, goals, motivation to achieve, and social behavior.

When an individual's experiences and interactions within the broader social order reinforce his and his group's perceptions, he may unwittingly accept his perceived status as "the way things are." The social and educational implications of this phenomenon are disastrous because education and learning primarily take place through constructive social interactions. When these social interactions take place within a social order that consciously or unconsciously accepts harmful, stereotypical characterizations and social stratification, both the teachers and their students are trapped in a perceived reality that denies each student's unique individuality. Within such a social construct, the assumptions a teacher makes about each student's culture stereotypes the student and prevents authentic teacher-student interaction and the student's individual construction of meaning, which as a result has a devastating effect on what the student learns and how he or she learns it.

It is obviously impossible for teachers and educational leaders to know everything about each cultural group they will encounter in their schools and classrooms. This insufficient knowledge often results in stereotypes and leads to distorted generalizations about students as culturally deprived because their cultural characteristics are different from those of the dominant culture. This perception of cultural deprivation often leads to assumptions about students being deficient culturally. Garcia (1999) points out that educators must respond to this dilemma by focusing on the intersection of the school's social context with the student's home and community contexts. He further suggests that for students from diverse cultures to feel included in the broader, comprehensive culture of the school, educators must begin to see cultural differences as added opportunities to strengthen learning rather than as deficiencies that must be filled with the dominant culture. Culturally proficient educational leaders take responsibility for helping each student understand himself or herself as a unique, competent, and valued member of a diverse cultural community rather than a deprived minority in a dominant culture.

The two conversations that follow illustrate the guiding principle of acknowledging and respecting unique cultural needs. In the first conversation, Maple View School District's administrative team is in its second day of an 8-day series of seminars focusing on culturally proficient leadership strategies. They have been working with Dr. Andrew Ramsey and Dr. Frederick Jackson, who are recognized throughout the state as conscientious and sensitive group facilitators who work primarily with district and school administrators intent on reshaping their districts and schools using the guiding principles of cultural proficiency as a constructive framework. In their first session with the Maple View team, the facilitators, "Andy" and "Fred," as they like to be called by the groups with which they work, concentrated on the continuum of cultural proficiency, the guiding principles, and the essential elements.

Toward the end of the first session, Andy and Fred asked the administrative team to interview at least 10 teachers and record their responses to the following questions and then to bring the interview data with them to the next session:

- Who are the underperforming students in our school? How would you describe them demographically?
- What adjectives would describe them as students?
- How would you describe their parents?
- How would you describe the neighborhoods where they live?
- How would you describe the language they speak at home?

Conversation 9: What Were You Expecting?

Dr. Barbara Campbell, the superintendent of the Maple View School District, and her administrative team are taking seriously their commitment to develop an organizational culture and behavior expectations that are consistent with the five guiding principles of culturally proficient practice. The principals have interviewed colleagues at their schools in an effort to comply with Dr. Campbell's assignment to describe obstacles to student achievement for each subgroup of students at their schools. These interview data are one of the indicators they will be using to guide their planning.

A group of the white principals were interested to see what, if any, stereotypes they would glean from their colleagues at their schools. Let's listen to the conversation that is emerging as the second day in the series begins:

Andy:	Well, as I look across the room at data arrayed on your tables, it's clear that you've collected a lot of information!
Tony Franklin (principal of Pine Hills Middle School):	You're right about that, Andy. This was an interesting assignment. I learned a lot just by asking my teachers the questions.
Fred:	Well, Tony, what are your findings?
Tony:	I learned some pretty interesting things, but right now I'm more interested in knowing why Sam has that astonished look on his face.
Sam Brewer (principal of Pine Hills High School):	I don't know if you're seeing astonishment or feelings of foolishness!
Andy:	Wow, Sam, that sounds pretty heavy. What's going on?
Sam:	Well, I'm feeling stupid. That's what's going on.
Fred:	Sam, we're all here to learn. The only stupidity would be closing ourselves off from looking at the data and learning from it.
Sam:	Well, this is actually kind of embarrassing. At Pine Hills High, we use a pretty derogatory name to identify a group of kids who come from that area across the highway where there's a lot of unemployment and people are really struggling financially.
Andy:	This is showing up in the data you collected?
Sam:	Yeah, I think that's why it hit me so hard. We refer to those kids as "the trailer park kids." Looking at my data spread out in front of me, I see that we use this label to pigeonhole and stereotype those kids. I can't believe I didn't see this before now.

Fred: That's why looking at this kind of real data is so important. It helps us see patterns of behavior that we just take for granted or overlook because it's "just what we do." It's that kind of unconscious stereotyping and the assumptions behind it that are so harmful. We stereotype the group and treat them as a solid block rather than a group of unique individuals.

Andy: Sam, your recognizing that stereotyping pattern in your data has helped all of us learn something very important.

This conversation reveals how assumptions about a cultural group such as the "trailer park kids" can transcend traditionally identified cultural groups and still stereotype all members of a group and keep them locked out of the opportunity to be academically and socially successful individuals. The assumptions and stereotypes that teachers have about the potential of a group and its capacity to be successful can cause them to react to all members of the group with generalized low expectations rather than responding to the unique individual potential and educational needs of each group member. Culturally proficient educational leaders must be vigilant in recognizing the deleterious impact of insensitive, thoughtless stereotyping of students and, moreover, must intervene with equal vigilance to ensure students an educational environment that is not culturally or socially detrimental to their individual success as learners.

Conversation 10: Let Their Culture Be Your Guide

In the following conversation, we look in on Dr. Frank Johnson, who has been a professor of educational administration at the Midland State University near Maple View for 11 years. He enjoys teaching and prides himself on his good working relationship with the students in his graduate level classes at Midland. Many of his students are beginning administrators from the Maple View School District, and Dr. Johnson is familiar with the current issues and activities going on in the district. Approximately 2 years ago, he and his family moved into a new home in Maple View, and they enjoy living in a suburban community with such a richly diverse population. Dr. Johnson has met with Dr. Barbara Campbell several times during the past 2 years, and he has offered her his assistance and support in the district. His children attend Pine Hills High

School, and he and his wife are active in parent activities at the school.

At the beginning of each semester, Dr. Johnson invites his students to his home for a potluck dinner. At the dinner, he encourages all his students to call him by his first name. This is very important to him symbolically. He wants to cultivate a collegial relationship with his students, and he hopes to work collaboratively with them on issues they are dealing with in their schools. He estimates that a majority of his students welcome his invitation, but he has noticed a subtle change in his classes during the past 2 years as the social and cultural demography of his students began to change. This evening, two of his students, Jorge Alvarenga and Jung Hai Kim, want to discuss his request and let him know how they feel about it:

Jung Hai: Dr. Johnson, Jorge and I want you to know that we truly appreciate your invitation to address you by your first name, but it's just not comfortable for us. We hope you're not offended.

Professor Johnson: Of course, not, that's why the invitation is to use either my first name or any of my titles, like doctor, professor, or even mister.

Jorge: What Jung Hai and I are trying to say is that it's disrespectful in our culture to address our teachers by their first names. Even though we were both raised in the United States, our cultural traditions are still strong.

Jung Hai: We'd feel like we were being rude to call you by your first name. I would feel embarrassed.

Jorge: I'd feel embarrassed, too. I hope you understand.

Professor Johnson: You know, when I asked you to call me by my first name, I didn't stop to think of the cultural implications. I wasn't consciously aware of how somebody raised in a culture different from mine might react. I was just thinking about my own cultural norms and unconsciously making an assumption that everyone would feel comfortable with my request. You both have helped me learn an important lesson about my assumptions. Thanks.

Jung Hai: You're welcome, Dr. Johnson. I wasn't sure how you'd respond to what we had to say, but Jorge said we should speak up or nothing will ever change, we won't be aware of one another's cultural comfort levels.

Jorge: Thanks for responding the way you did, Dr. Johnson. We learned a lot from the way you handled this. I think I'll be braver the next time something like this happens.

The common factor in these two conversations is the way the people having the conversations recognized the impact of their assumptions on others and then took care to respond with sensitivity to the unique cultural needs expressed in the dialogue. The recognition of our assumptions and stereotypes is a powerful first step in identifying and then responding thoughtfully and respectfully to the unique cultural needs of people from social and cultural groups that are different from our own.

■ Reflective Activity

Think about your own assumptions and stereotypes about people from cultures other than yours or about students whose living situations may be much different from yours. How do assumptions and stereotypes block you from responding thoughtfully and respectfully toward others?

_____

_____

_____

_____

_____

_____

Now, put your knowledge to use. During the next several days, look at how people in your school or office address issues of culture. Note levels of comfort with conversation about culture and diversity. Observe how people describe their colleagues, students, and members of the community who are culturally different from them. Pay attention to how they describe people who speak languages other than English. Monitor how you describe those who are culturally different from you. The adjectives you and your colleagues use will give you insight to each of your values in this area. After a few days, ask yourself: "What am I learning about my colleagues and about me?" "In what ways do the guiding principles guide us in identifying obstacles to student achievement?"

3

The Cultural Proficiency Continuum

The Inside-Out Process to Becoming Culturally Proficient

Being able to put aside one's self-centered focus and impulses has social benefits: It opens the way to empathy, to real listening, to taking another person's perspective. Empathy . . . leads to caring, altruism, and compassion. Seeing things from another's perspective breaks down biased stereotypes, and so breeds tolerance and acceptance of differences. These capacities are ever more called on in our increasingly pluralistic society, allowing people to live together in mutual respect and creating the possibility of productive public discourse. These are the basic arts of democracy.

—Daniel Goleman (1995, p. 285)

We send emotional signals in every encounter, and those signals affect the people we are with, whether or not we are aware of our impact. Conscious attention to how our behavior makes another person feel—for instance, sad, rejected, scared, and incompetent or happy, accepted, safe, and productive—is an example of interpersonal competence that enables us to interact with other people effectively and responsively. Self-management combined with empathy for others helps us to analyze and control our own emotional dispositions and reactions and our resulting behaviors in terms of both their personal and their social benefit. These basic social competences or "people skills" enable us to shape effective interactions, make meaningful connections, and recognize and respond to people's feelings and concerns. More than ever before, the growing diversity and increasing pluralism of our schools require educational leaders to be socially competent in ways that demonstrate respect, mutual understanding, justice, and concern for students who are culturally unlike them—students who differ racially and ethnically, students who speak different languages, students who have different beliefs, and students who have different ways of expressing their cultural distinctiveness. It is probably not possible for an educational leader to know every important aspect of each of the diverse cultures represented in most American public schools today. The culturally proficient response to this dilemma is to seek and develop the knowledge, skills, and attitudes that demonstrate openness and authentic responsiveness to the heritage, values, and expressions of each cultural group represented in the student population. To lead successfully now, as discussed in Chapter 2, leaders also must consistently model socially competent attitudes, values, and dispositions by demonstrating interactions that are shaped by understanding and embracing the five principles of cultural proficiency as core leadership values.

Understanding and acknowledging the five principles of cultural proficiency, described in Chapter 2, and choosing to manifest them in your behavior are demonstrations of culturally proficient leadership. The choice you make to align your leadership actions with the five principles of cultural proficiency communicates a strong message throughout your school's community that you value diversity and fully expect that every individual will do the same. Indeed, the guiding principles are attitudinal benchmarks that enable you and others to assess progress toward acknowledging and valuing cultural differences, and although this assessment yields crucial information, it is insufficient by itself in provoking the development of culturally proficient behaviors.

Cultural Proficiency: A Transformative Approach

Cultural proficiency is an inside-out perspective on change in which school leaders transform approaches to their personal leadership behaviors and to their school practices. Leaders who manifest cultural proficiency guide their colleagues to examine personal values and behaviors in such a way that the members of the school realize that it is they who must adapt their practices to meet the needs of the students and the community they serve. Likewise, these leaders support their colleagues and members of the community in aligning the school's policies, practices, and procedures to achieve cultural proficiency (Lindsey, Nuri Robins, & Terrell, 2003; Nuri Robins, Lindsey, Lindsey, & Terrell, 2002).

The Cultural Proficiency Continuum

As a leader, making a commitment to align your practice with culturally proficient behavior and working to engage others in making similar commitments require that you begin where you are—individually and organizationally. The cultural proficiency continuum is a tool that offers you a contextual frame of reference that is useful in examining and analyzing your responses to issues of diversity. From an organizational perspective, the continuum provides a means of assessing how your school or district deals with cultural differences. It also can assist you and others to examine and evaluate how your organization initiates, implements, and enforces policies and practices that represent its position on issues of diversity.

The continuum describes a range of behaviors from *destructiveness*, the denial and suppression of a people's culture, to *proficiency*, the acknowledgment and elevation of all cultures (see Figure 3.1). The behaviors identified on the continuum are not fixed points; rather, each descriptive point represents an array of practices and policies that characterize a developmental stage or phase of social competence.

As an educational leader, it is essential to recognize that responses and reactions to students' cultural identities have a profound influence on what students learn and how they learn it. Furthermore, a leader's responses and reactions to difference, whether conscious or unconscious, can be manifested in several ways that range from devastating

Figure 3.1   The Cultural Proficiency Continuum

Cultural Destructiveness		Cultural Blindness		Cultural Competence	
	Cultural Incapacity		Cultural Precompetence		Cultural Proficiency

a student's sense of cultural identity to maximizing and enlarging a student's uniqueness. The range of these responses is represented in the cultural proficiency continuum (Cross, 1989; Lindsey, Nuri Robins, & Terrell, 1999):

- *Cultural destructiveness:* negating, disparaging, or purging cultures that are different from your own.
- *Cultural incapacity:* elevating the superiority of your own cultural values and beliefs and suppressing cultures that are different from your own.
- *Cultural blindness:* acting as if differences among cultures do not exist and refusing to recognize any differences.
- *Cultural precompetence:* recognizing that lack of knowledge, experience, and understanding of other cultures limits your ability to effectively interact with them.
- *Cultural competence:* employing any policy, practice, or behavior that uses the essential elements of cultural proficiency on behalf of the school or the district. Cultural competence is interacting with other cultural groups in ways that recognize and value their differences, motivate you to assess your own skills, expand your knowledge and resources, and, ultimately, cause you to adapt your relational behavior.
- *Cultural proficiency:* honoring the differences among cultures, seeing diversity as a benefit, and interacting knowledgeably and respectfully among a variety of cultural groups.

The continuum can be useful and instructive as a tool to assess growth toward cultural proficiency. Used as a gauge, it can yield a realistic appraisal of both your personal and your organizational development toward proficient cultural practices. Most important, the continuum can help you determine where to begin—that is, where you are. To begin with yourself is an inside-out process of self-examination, evaluation, and awareness. In such a process, you become self-conscious in the best sense. To begin with yourself calls on you to make an authentic assessment of your assumptions, attitudes, dispositions, and behaviors. Which phase on the continuum would best characterize your stage of development? What about your organization? Where along the continuum would you place your organization's (school's or district's) policies and practices? The complexity of the task is hidden in the simplicity of the question.

■ Reflective Activity

Become self-conscious. Consider how you respond and react to displays of cultural distinctiveness and expression that are different from your own sense of cultural identity. Think of a recent situation during which you encountered such an experience. What signals did you communicate?

_____

_____

_____

_____

_____

_____

Movement along the continuum will not be a smooth journey on which you glide continually forward in the right direction. Your progress toward competence and proficiency, like your learning, may be a rocky, bumpy ride at times. Sometimes you will lurch forward and then slide backward, sometimes you may stall, and sometimes the road will smooth out before you and you will make great progress. The decision to learn and grow and change is yours to make.

■ Return to Maple View

In the following brief fictional episodes, we return to the Maple View School District to examine some everyday school interactions that illustrate the six points of the continuum. The situations described are simulations of authentic experiences we have had in schools in which we have worked. Following each of the interactions is a set of questions that will guide you in your learning at three levels: Analyze the vignette, describe the behavior, and identify the underlying assumptions implicit in the particular situation.

Episode 1: It's Not My Job!

> *Cultural destructiveness* is any action that negates, dispar-
> ages, or purges cultural practices or expressions of culture
> that are different from your own; it may be manifested
> through an organization's policies and practices or through
> an individual's assumptions and behavior.

Cultural destructiveness has its basis in historical acts of oppression, whether racism, sexism, heterosexism, or any other "-ism."
The history of our country has been one of a slowly unfolding
democracy. Initially, voting and property rights were almost solely
the domains of propertied white men. The struggles to eliminate
African slavery, Native American apartheid, Jim Crow segregation,
Japanese American internment, and the second-class status of
women are among the many vital parts of our history that are rarely
visible in our schools' curricula. The effect of this omission is
twofold. First, it deprives educators and their students of a context
by which to understand the disparities that exist in today's schools
(Loewen, 1995). Without this context for understanding the disparities that exist in society, it is too easy to ascribe cause to being a lack
of initiative or will. Second, it fails to "show the numerous benefits
that members of the dominant group have derived from the subju-
gation of other people" (Nuri Robins et al., 2002, p. 93).

Whether intentional or not, the effect of culturally destructive
school leaders' behaviors or school's practices has the effect of deny-
ing nondominant groups legitimacy in the school setting. Out-and-
out racist, sexist, or heterosexist behaviors and school policies and
practices are, no doubt, readily visible. However, there are behaviors,
policies, and practices that create and perpetuate disparate treatment
in our classrooms and schools that are invisible to the educator but are
quite obvious to those most directly affected by the acts. It is this latter
set of behaviors and policies that are addressed in the first episode.

The first situation involves members of the faculty at Maple View
Middle School who are working with Alfredo Crawford, a recognized
expert in instructional strategies for English language acquisition. As
you read this episode, look for the indications of culturally destructive
behavior and the assumptions that such behavior reveals.

Maple View Middle School has been experiencing demographic
shifts in its student population for the past several years. Many of the

students now attending the school are identified as English language learners. Faced with this new reality, some teachers have taken the initiative to earn second-language instruction authorizations. In most cases, the recently credentialed teachers learned effective second-language instructional strategies through their university coursework. They have inspired some of the more experienced teachers to use the new, more effective techniques. However, there is some resistance, as you will see by this conversation at a recent staff development session.

Dr. Crawford was beginning to introduce an activity in today's professional development session when Ira Robinson, a seventh-grade math instructor, stood up with his arms folded across his chest. In an argumentative tone, but with a smile on his face, Ira interjects,

Ira Robinson:	Mr. Crawford, or is it Dr. Crawford? Are you going to tell us again that we're not doing our jobs here—that is, we're not doing a good job?
Alfredo Crawford:	Well, first please call me "Alfredo," or "Mr. Crawford" or "Dr. Crawford." I'm comfortable with any of them. Now, what makes you think I am going to criticize your work?
Ira:	We hear it every time they bring somebody in to talk to us. Ever since the students began to change, all we've heard around here is that we're doing a lousy job. We hear it every year from the principal when the test scores come out. But never, never do we hear what the parents need to do. They're the ones who are responsible.
Alfredo:	I hear a lot of frustration in what you're saying, Ira—or . . . Mr. Robinson. What I plan to do today is share some interesting new strategies and approaches that should make your teaching more effective and remove some of that frustration you're feeling.
Ira (sitting down angrily):	Well, Dr. Crawford, I find that insulting! I've been teaching math here for 23 years, and you're going to tell me that I don't know what I'm doing. The problem isn't my teaching "strategy," as you put it. The problem is these kids who don't

	speak English. I know how to teach math. I'm not an English teacher.
Alfredo (standing silently for a moment):	When you and I earned our teaching credentials, there were relatively few immigrant students in our schools. During our careers, that has changed substantially. Now we've got the responsibility to teach students who have limited or no English skills.
Ira:	Well, there are a lot of us here who don't believe it's our job to be an induction center for immigrants. If these people want to be in this country, let them learn the language before coming here! As for me, I'm a math teacher. It's not my job to teach English, or for that matter, what you call "language acquisition skills."

■ Reflective Activity

How is cultural destructiveness displayed in this vignette? What is the culturally destructive behavior?

_____

_____

_____

_____

_____

_____

What assumptions is Mr. Robinson making?

_____

_____

_____

_____

_____

As the school's principal, how would you seek to mediate this situation?

_____

_____

_____

_____

_____

_____

Episode 2: Shiny Red Apples

> *Cultural incapacity* is any action that elevates the superiority of your own cultural values and beliefs while suppressing cultures that are different from your own.

Cultural incapacity is any policy, practice, or behavior that venerates one culture over all others. Such policies, practices, or behaviors can influence the worldviews of members of both the dominant and the nondominant groups. The history of our country is replete with examples of official acts of cultural incapacity, such as the restrictive immigration and Jim Crow laws of the 19th and 20th centuries. Laws such as these helped systematize the belief in the superiority of the dominant group and the inherent inferiority of subordinate groups. The combination of laws and concomitant beliefs among members of the dominant group gives rise to discriminatory practices, lowered expectations, and subtle messages to people that they are not valued (Nuri Robins et al., 2002). Freire (1987, 1999) discussed the net effect of these behavior and practices as being internalized oppression when members of nondominant groups assume the worldview of the dominant group to be true.

In the previous discussion of cultural destructiveness, we pointed out that the negative effect of a behavior, practice, or policy that is demeaning had little or no relationship to one's intentionality. The same is true for cultural incapacity. To the student, parent, community member, or colleague, when a person becomes an object and not a fully functioning person through another person's prejudice, bias, stereotyping, or indifference, it all feels the same. The net effect for the person on the receiving end of the behavior, practice, or policy may range from anger to resistance and learned helplessness.

In the second situation, we visit the classroom of Mrs. Dorothy Jackson, a teacher at Maple View Elementary School who, along with other teachers at the school, has been working with Dr. Laura Ruiz, a reading and language arts consultant from the regional Comprehensive School Reform Center. As you read this episode, look for the indications of behavior that culturally incapacitates specific groups of students, and identify the assumptions that this behavior reveals.

Dr. Ruiz has asked Anne Browning, the Maple View School District's language arts coordinator, to accompany her on today's visit to Maple View Elementary. Dr. Ruiz has been working with the teachers in grade level groups to help them improve their writing instruction. The school's Hispanic and African American students, particularly the boys in these groups, have not demonstrated adequate progress in English composition and generative writing skills. She is spending the week visiting classrooms. Last week, she met with the school's leadership team and agreed with them that she should familiarize herself with the culture of the school and classrooms to be most helpful in coaching teachers to strengthen their writing programs and improve their instructional strategies. Today, we go along with Laura and Anne as they begin their visit to Dorothy Jackson's fourth-grade classroom.

Laura and Anne arrive at the classroom at approximately 10 a.m. and find it abuzz with activity. As she enters the classroom, Laura quickly scans the environment for examples of students' work. A colorful bulletin board on the rear wall displays a large apple tree made of construction paper. On one side of the tree is a heading that reads "The Red Apples," and on the other side is a heading that reads "The Green Apples." Laura observes that both sides display apples with children's names on them, and she wonders what criteria are used to determine the placement of apples.

As the two visitors enter the classroom, Dorothy Jackson interrupts the class to introduce Dr. Ruiz and Ms. Browning to the students:

Dorothy (greeting the two visitors at the door and smiling in a welcoming way): Class, this is Dr. Ruiz and Ms. Browning. Dr. Ruiz is the person I was telling you about. She is going to help us improve our writing here at Maple View. If you recall, yesterday I told you that Dr. Ruiz was going to visit our classroom and watch how we learn to write. Remember?

Laura (smiling and walking into the classroom):	Good morning class. Mrs. Jackson is right. I'm here to learn from you by observing how you do your work and watching to see what helps you learn. I don't want to interrupt you, so please go back to your work. Ms. Browning and I will be very quiet so that we don't bother you. (The two women walk to the rear of the classroom.)
Dorothy:	Well, first Dr. Ruiz and Ms. Browning, let me introduce my wonderful fourth graders. We are working on a writing assignment this morning. These students (gesturing to a group of girls) are my shining red apples. They have already finished the assignment and are doing some enrichment work. Their stories are just wonderful. This group (gesturing to another group of mostly Hispanic and African American boys) we call the green apples. They have a long way to go before they turn red. This is the group that needs your help.

Laura's heart sank as she listened to Dorothy's introduction. She glanced at Anne and saw that she also was disturbed by the teacher's words. The students carried on with their work as if nothing unusual had occurred. The effect of Dorothy's comments may not be readily discernible in the moment, but most assuredly, they will have a cumulative effect on both groups of students.

■ Reflective Activity

How is cultural incapacity displayed in this episode? What is the culturally incompetent behavior? Who is incapacitated?

_____

_____

_____

_____

_____

_____

How would you describe the expectations Mrs. Jackson has of her learners? What information reveals her expectations?

_____

_____

_____

_____

_____

How might different groups of students in Mrs. Jackson's class variously judge their own capabilities? Why?

_____

_____

_____

_____

_____

As a school leader, how would you work with Mrs. Jackson?

_____

_____

_____

_____

_____

_____

Episode 3: They All Look Alike to Me

Cultural blindness is any policy, practice, or behavior that ignores existing cultural differences or that considers such differences inconsequential.

Cultural blindness is a vexing point on the continuum in that there is often a difference between what is stated and how the statement is experienced. The blindness is in the speaker not being able to hear how others are receiving the statements. The blindness is in the speaker being mystified or angry that he or she was misunderstood. The dominant culture in our country has placed a value on cultural blindness. You can see it in many of our instructional materials. When there are faces of color, they are most often in the context of middle-class and upper-middle-class experiences. Similarly, much of our history and language arts materials revolve around heroic themes that show how people have benefited from struggles as if all one had to do to overcome one's lot in life was to work a little harder or, at least, not be so sensitive.

The third situation involves Maureen Bailey, the newly appointed principal at Rose Garden Elementary School, who is meeting with her faculty group after visiting every classroom in the school. The Rose Garden faculty has been working together for the past 5 years to create an interdisciplinary project-based curriculum that integrates language arts and social studies. As you read this episode, look for the indications of behavior that ignores existing cultural differences among groups of students and the assumptions that this behavior reveals.

Maureen Bailey has had the good fortune to work as an educator in several different settings. She began as a teacher in the Department of Defense Schools, which gave her many exciting opportunities to teach in Western Europe, Turkey, Korea, and Central America. For the past 8 years, she has worked in the Maple View School District, first as a teacher for 5 years and then later as an assistant principal. This year, she has been promoted to the position of principal at Rose Garden Elementary School, one of the older school facilities in Maple View. Rose Garden is located on the east side of the district and draws students from a community that is richly diverse both culturally and economically. The school has earned a reputation throughout the county for its tradition of recognizing, respecting, and celebrating the many racial, sociocultural, and linguistic customs and traditions of its students and their families. During the past 5 years, the teachers at Rose Garden have worked together in grade level clusters to develop a schoolwide project-based language arts and social studies curriculum that engages students in learning and applying content standards within the context of their own and other students' heritages. Many parents—even those who have full-time jobs—volunteer their time and contribute traditional artifacts so that students can learn about diverse cultures from authentic sources. Rose Garden's curriculum is exemplary, and many teachers from other districts visit the school to observe how the teachers plan and develop their innovative curriculum in teams and how they use the curriculum with their students.

Soon after school resumed in September, Maureen announced to the faculty that she would be visiting each classroom, attending every curriculum-planning meeting, speaking with each teacher, and interviewing some students to learn more about what was going on in the school. Now, on an afternoon in early October, Maureen has chosen her third meeting with the faculty to share her observations. The faculty has gathered in the school's library to hear her report:

Maureen Bailey (standing in front of the group holding a sheaf of papers):	I'm so happy to be the principal at this school! You're all such professionals, and you're doing such good work with these children—even with all the challenges you face every day.
Maxine Cho (raising her hand and then speaking when Maureen acknowledges her):	Thanks, Maureen! I'm impressed that you made it to every classroom already. But what I really want to know is: What's your impression of the rich diversity at this school? I mean, as you visited the classrooms, what were some of the things students from different ethnic groups were doing? What impressions did you take away from that?
Maureen:	Well, when I look at the school as a whole, the diversity is incredible. But, I think what I've noticed most, after visiting every classroom and watching the students doing their work, is that I can't tell you the ethnic, racial, or gender makeup of the students in your classrooms. I really don't see color. They all look like little Americans to me, and I think that's great!
Maxine (stunned and silent for several seconds):	Mrs. Bailey, I'm surprised to hear your response. As you know, here at Rose Garden we have been working extremely hard to acknowledge and respect each of the groups represented in our student population. We are committed to recognizing the unique characteristics and contributions of each of the groups represented in our student population.

■ Reflective Activity

How is cultural blindness displayed in this episode? Why is this culturally incompetent behavior?

_____

_____

_____

_____

_____

What are the assumptions that underlie this cultural blindness?

_____

_____

_____

_____

_____

How is cultural blindness a deterrent to successful learning?

_____

_____

_____

_____

_____

How might you advise or coach Maxine Cho and the other teachers in the school to respond to Maureen Bailey? Why?

_____

_____

_____

_____

_____

_____

As a district leader, how would you work with Maureen?

_____

_____

_____

_____

_____

_____

Episode 4: No Excuses

> *Culturally precompetent* people and organizations recognize that their skills and practices are limited when interacting with other cultural groups.

Cultural precompetence is people beginning to know what they do not know. The culturally precompetent educator has at least a basic understanding of his or her own culture and the awareness that his or her school has a distinct organizational culture. The culturally precompetent educator has begun the shift from talking about educational disparities as something being wrong with *them* to *our practice* needing to be adapted for use with new groups. The culturally precompetent educator has begun to see that the dominant group is handicapped in what it does not know about interacting with groups other than their own. Very often, a hallmark of the culturally precompetent educator is frustration in knowing that current practices are not effective but not knowing what to do about it. This can be a point of readiness to learn.

The fourth situation portrays a group of teachers on the academic planning team at Maple View High School. For several weeks, they have been meeting with Connie Hampton, Maple View's assistant principal, to review and analyze their latest student performance data in relation to their expectations for their students. As you read this episode, look for the indications of members of the group beginning to realize their limitations regarding their students' backgrounds and cultural experiences. What are the assumptions this behavior reveals?

Ten years ago, Maple View High School was recognized as having one of the most "rigorous" secondary academic programs in the county. Test scores have declined steadily during the past decade. Many in the school district cite the shift in student demographics as being the cause for the decline in test scores. The student body now consists of recent immigrants from Mexico, Central America, Asia, and Middle Eastern countries. Less than half of the students are from middle-income families, and most others are from lower-income families, for which opportunities for formal education beyond that provided by the school have been limited.

The school's administrators, in an effort to provide support for immigrant students, gradually dropped much of their rigorous curriculum in favor of an increasing number of English-as-a-second language and remedial math classes. They believed that the students must be proficient in English and basic computation skills to be successful in this country. However, the scores continued the downward trend.

A small core of rigorous courses and "advanced placement" classes were continuing to serve approximately 18% of the students who were able to meet the high expectations of their teachers. This small cluster of students could compete academically with students from any other high school in the county, and they were the source of much school pride on the part of the school's administrators.

The downward cycle of test scores caused the school to qualify for state funds to address the needs of students. The academic planning team, in consultation with an external evaluator, has been engaged in examining student test scores along with other indicators of student achievement.

Today, Dr. Hampton is meeting with the teachers on the team, and she is just completing a guided review of the test scores for the past 3 years. This is the third session in which the academic planning team has been examining these data:

Connie Hampton (turning off the overhead projector):	Okay, we've been looking at these data for over 3 weeks now, and we've been looking at the ways the school's curriculum meets or doesn't meet the needs of all of our students. What patterns are you seeing today?
Josh Turner (a young biology teacher, quickly responds):	Well, the first time we looked at all these reports, I wondered to myself: Wow, how can we expect anything different from kids whose parents don't value education? Now, I am at a different place.
Irene Thompson (school counselor and chair of the faculty senate):	Me, too, and I can't figure out why and where. It seems so strange.
Josh:	Well, I've been thinking a lot about a question you asked at our last meeting, Connie. You asked us something like—let me know if I get this right.
Connie:	I will, Josh. Go on.
Josh:	Okay, last week, when we were looking at the family background data, I said I thought many of our parents are poorly educated. You agreed, but followed with, "What can you do differently that will make a difference in our students' learning?" Somehow, it doesn't seem like you responded to my comment. Am I missing something?
Irene:	Yes, that's what I heard, too!
Connie:	So, Josh and Irene, you both heard my question, and you've been thinking about it all week. What did that question mean for you?
Josh (smiling a little anxiously):	Well, this isn't very comfortable, and it won't be easy, but the past week I've been thinking that we're the ones who have to change what we're doing if we want our students to learn what we expect them to learn.

Irene (nodding in agreement):	Do you remember what you said at our first meeting, Connie? I've been thinking about it a lot. You said there are no excuses for not teaching our students. I've been thinking about that. "No excuses" means we have to find new ways to teach our students what they need to know.
Josh:	Yes, that's what's been rattling around in my brain all week, too. We have no excuses.

■ Reflective Activity

How is cultural precompetence displayed in this episode? What are the individuals in the situation learning?

_____

_____

_____

_____

_____

_____

How would you describe the expectations that Connie Hampton has for the teachers at Maple View High? What information reveals her expectations?

_____

_____

_____

_____

_____

_____

If you were Connie, how would you continue working with Josh and Irene and the other teachers in the group?

_____

_____

_____

_____

_____

_____

What do you see as the challenges for this group, and how would you coach them?

_____

_____

_____

_____

_____

_____

Episode 5: Bridges Among Cultures

Cultural competence is any policy, practice, or behavior that uses the essential elements of cultural proficiency for the individual or the organization. The essential elements are

- Assessing culture
- Valuing diversity
- Managing the dynamics of difference
- Adapting to diversity
- Institutionalizing cultural knowledge

Culturally competent school leaders use the five essential elements as standards for their personal and organizational planning. These leaders are students of themselves and the culture of their schools. Culturally competent school leaders take the responsibility and opportunity to use the five essential elements as leverage points for improving current practices in order that educators, students, parents, and community members are in an environment in which continuous improvement is fundamental to the school vision.

The fifth episode depicts the work of a district task force that is assessing and analyzing the district's middle school social studies curriculum. Maple View's superintendent, Dr. Barbara Campbell, has selected Anthony (Tony) Franklin, the principal at Pine Hills Middle School, to chair the district's Middle Grades Social Studies Standards Task Force. Dr. Campbell wants Tony and the other members of the task force to assess how well the district's middle school social studies curriculum aligns with the state's Social Studies Standards. She also has asked the task force for an assessment of how well the district's and the state's standards align with the principles of cultural proficiency that are guiding all curriculum development in the district. The task force includes new and experienced teachers, two administrators, a school counselor, and parents from the district's Community Cultural Proficiency Council. As you read this episode, watch for indications of behavior that demonstrate cultural competence. What evidence of cultural competence can you find in the episode?

Today's task force session is the second meeting for the group. Sitting around the table today are Tony, the chair; Helene Kim, a seventh-grade history teacher; Jackie Sims, a sixth-grade social studies teacher in her second year; Francisco Alvarado, the assistant principal at Maple View Middle School; Lucy Tyrell, the counselor at Pine Hills Middle School; and Kwame Randolph, the parent of two middle school students at Maple View and cochair of the Community Cultural Proficiency Council. They are waiting for a few more task force members before they begin. Tony is energized and anxious to get the meeting started. He has brought copies of the standards along with copies of the five principles of cultural proficiency:

Tony Franklin (distributing the copies around the table):	I'd like to get started. We have a lot to do, and this is a very important task, one that is going to take considerable time and study.
Helene Kim (nodding in agreement):	You're so right, Tony. I feel very honored to be on this task force.

Jackie Sims:	Oh, me too. And as a new teacher, I'm so grateful for the opportunity to work with all of you on this important task. I'm so pleased to have Lucy on our team. Lucy has been a social studies teacher at both Pine Hills and Maple View. In her role as counselor, she remains the one most knowledgeable about the breadth and depth of our curriculum.
Helene:	She's also on the district's Community Cultural Proficiency Council.
Kwame Randolph (agreeing with Helene):	It seems to me that a good beginning might be to hear Lucy's assessment of our district curriculum. So, Lucy, just how balanced is our curriculum? In other words, what do you see as our strong points, and what are the points of omission?
Lucy Tyrell (after a moment of reflection):	I'm very comfortable with that as a starting point, but I want to let you know that I've got blind spots, too. For instance, the events of September 11 have shown me how little I know about the Middle East, the Muslim religion, or our country's formal and informal policies that impact these issues. One of the things I see coming from this study is that even though our district has no Middle Eastern or Muslim students that I'm aware of, how important it is for our curriculum to be inclusive.
Francisco Alvarado:	Yes, the new state standards for social studies are very explicit about our students being prepared to live and function in an interdependent, global world. Lucy, I'm sure that your blind spot is one that many of us share. That kind of openness is what we need as we begin this work.
Lucy:	You're so right, Francisco. We need to make sure that our district's social studies curriculum builds bridges for our students to learn about and recognize the many diverse cultural groups among us.
Tony (smiling broadly):	That's it! That's what our work is all about. We're building bridges among us, among our cultures.

■ Reflective Activity

How is culturally competent behavior displayed in this episode? What example stands out for you?

_____

_____

_____

_____

_____

_____

What are some of the assumptions held by participants in this episode? What evidence is included in the episode?

_____

_____

_____

_____

_____

_____

What do you think Dr. Barbara Campbell envisions as the next steps for this group? If you got the opportunity, how might you coach her?

_____

_____

_____

_____

_____

_____

Episode 6: Change Your Calendar

> *Cultural proficiency* is knowing how to learn and teach about different groups in ways that acknowledge and honor all people and the groups they represent.

Cultural proficiency is a way of being alert and aware as a leader. Cultural proficiency is manifest in organizations and people who esteem cultures, who continually learn about individuals and organizational cultures, and who interact effectively with a variety of cultural groups. The culturally proficient leader acknowledges the interrelatedness of personal, organizational, and cultural learning. Advocacy is a distinguishing characteristic of the culturally proficient leader. The culturally proficient leader advocates for people because it is the right and moral thing to do irrespective of whether or not the subjects of the advocacy are in the room at the time.

The school leadership team at Maple View Middle School was working with the assistant principal, Francisco Alvarado, to generate a curriculum-planning calendar. To have accurate information for the calendar, they decided to track and monitor the attendance patterns of all their students to schedule important curriculum units during the times of the year when most of the students are present. As you read this episode, look for examples of culturally proficient behavior among the team members.

Among several distinct patterns, the team's data revealed that many students of Mexican ancestry, especially those who had come to the United States recently, were absent around the times of cultural events such as Christmas and Easter. The pattern showed that for the past several years, large numbers of students and their families had regularly returned to Mexico to visit their families and celebrate religious and other cultural events. It was not unusual for students to return from Christmas and Easter visits with families in Mexico having missed a total of 3 weeks of classroom work, a situation that placed them far behind other students. This situation too often caused misery for both the students and the teachers.

The administrators and teachers at Maple View had asked the parents to not take their children out of school for such long periods of time. The school had worked with parents to help them understand the educational practices of their new country so that they would have their children back when school resumed. The strong cultural pull of family celebrations seemed to be stronger than the cultural tradition of the school calendar. The teachers even tried creating homework alternatives so the children could keep up with their schoolwork during these important family events. Their efforts were met with mixed results.

Today, the team is meeting to assess the results of their campaign to keep students in their classrooms. Sarah Chainey, a sixth-grade science teacher, is facilitating the meeting. Other members of the team include Helene Kim, a seventh-grade social studies teacher; Ron Sumii, an eighth-grade algebra teacher; and Jocelyn Donaldson, a seventh-grade language arts teacher. Francisco Alvarado, the school's assistant principal, also joined the group:

Sarah Chainey (displaying an overhead of the data):	So, as you see here, we've had this pattern of student absences every December and April. It's so frustrating because the kids are missing out on so much.
Ron Sumii:	Yep! The kids are right on target through the fall and into December. Then, bam, they're gone for 3 weeks. They fall behind and they never catch up. Their parents need to respect our school calendar.
Francisco Alvarado:	Sarah, you say the kids are missing out on so much. What would they miss if they didn't go back to Mexico to visit their families? For these kids, family is the center of their culture.
Jocelyn Donaldson:	I think you're right, Francisco. What if we change our calendar? Is that a possibility? Can we do that?
Francisco:	Our school calendar has to be 183 school days. Working with that total, we could organize our calendar so that the kids wouldn't fall behind in their schoolwork.
Sarah (turning off the projector):	Jocelyn, you're brilliant!
Helene Kim:	Wait, Sarah. Put that overhead up again. We can use it to plot our new calendar.

Ron: That's right. Now let's see, we need to plot our 183 days around these two blocks of time when the kids are in Mexico.

Finally, it dawned on the leadership team that the school was organized around the living patterns of students and families who had long ago migrated from the area. They decided they that could demonstrate respect for the families in the school's attendance area and organize the school calendar around their lifestyles, in much the same way their predecessors had generations before. With this new insight, the leadership team proposed that the school calendar be organized to fit the lifestyle patterns of the families the school was serving. Now, the school is closed for winter break for 4 weeks in late December and early January and for 2 weeks during the observance of Passion and Easter weeks. Once the decision was made and the calendar change was instituted, Sarah Chainey was heard explaining the Maple View teacher's accomplishment to a group of teachers from another school:

> You know, once we decided that the school calendar was created by people to serve their needs generations ago and was not etched in stone, it was pretty easy to get our priorities in order and decide how we could best meet the needs of our communities. Pretty neat, huh!

■   Reflective Activity

How is culturally proficient behavior depicted in this episode? What is one small, individual example you can describe?

_____

_____

_____

_____

_____

_____

How do the assumptions of the participants in this episode shift? What stimulates the shift?

_____

_____

_____

_____

_____

_____

If you were coaching this team, what next steps would you advise them to take?

_____

_____

_____

_____

_____

_____

What do you envision for this team as they continue their progress toward becoming culturally proficient?

_____

_____

_____

_____

_____

_____

In Chapters 2 and 3, you have become acquainted with two important tools: the five guiding principles of culturally proficient practice and the six points on the cultural proficiency continuum. Chapter 4 will guide you toward a deeper understanding of culturally proficient behavior by introducing the five elements of cultural proficiency. Before you move on, take a few moments to reflect on your own goals in relation to becoming more culturally proficient. What do you want your behavior to communicate to others? What signals do you want to send to people whose cultural identity is different from yours?

_____

_____

_____

_____

_____

_____

4

Standards for Leadership Behavior

The Five Essential Elements

In order to progress toward this goal, several current assumptions about equity and schooling must be challenged and changed to move the focus from diversity to equity and from tolerance to transformation.

—Stephanie Graham
and Randall Lindsey (2002, p. 23)

Culturally competent school leaders understand that effective leadership in a diverse environment is about changing the manner in which we work with those who are culturally different from ourselves. Personal transformation that facilitates organizational change is the goal of cultural competence.

Leading effectively in a diverse environment is not about changing others; it is about our own personal work. To guide the personal work in which school leaders examine their own values and behaviors and, in due time, the policies and practices of the school, the five essential elements of cultural competence serve as standards for culturally competent leadership. The essential elements of culturally competent school leadership are as follows (Lindsey, Nuri Robins, & Terrell, 2003; Nuri Robins, Lindsey, Lindsey, & Terrell, 2002):

- Assesses culture: Claim your differences.
- Values diversity: Name the differences.
- Manages the dynamics of difference: Frame the conflicts caused by differences.
- Adapts to diversity: Change to make a difference.
- Institutionalize cultural knowledge: Teach about differences.

As you read this chapter, review the assumptions for each point of the continuum that you identified in Chapter 3. Reviewing those assumptions will serve you in two ways. First, in reflecting on your assumptions, you will better understand the behaviors along the continuum and develop an even deeper appreciation for how our decisions as school leaders affect students. Second, after reading this chapter, you will know if your assumptions are consistent with the standards embodied in the five essential elements of cultural competence. At that point, you will have the opportunity to be intentional in choosing to integrate the essential elements into your professional practice.

The cultural competence continuum is composed of six points. The three points on the left side of the continuum focus on the behaviors and perceived motivation of others, whereas the three points on the right side of the continuum focus on personal behaviors and motives as school leaders. Importantly, the transition between cultural blindness and cultural precompetence serves as a tipping point or shift in thinking (Gladwell, 2000). As leaders, a shift in thinking occurs when we turn our attention from our interpretation of the behavior and motivation of others to an introspective look at our own behavior, values, and motives. School leaders who experience this shift in thinking examine their and the district's policies and practices to discover or devise ways in which to better serve their diverse communities. School leaders with whom we have worked describe this shift as being from the paralysis associated with cultural blindness to the empowerment involved with examining their own practices as school leaders.

Tolerance Versus Equity

During the school years 1999 and 2000, nine superintendents from Los Angeles and San Bernardino Counties met to study the achievement gaps within their schools. They invited the equity consultant from the Los Angeles County Office of Education and an author of this book to serve as resource persons and to facilitate the meetings. In time, they assumed the title of Superintendents' Collaborative for School Equity and Achievement. These superintendents were very knowledgeable about the dynamics affecting the achievement gap. They knew that having low-achieving students simply work harder was not the answer to closing the achievement gap. They knew that the answer to closing the achievement gap involved the intricate interplay of educator and system assumptions, expectations, and cultural issues (Graham & Lindsey, 2002).

In adapting the cultural proficiency approach to devising ways to close the achievement gap, the members of the Superintendents' Collaborative made clear distinctions in their use of the five essential elements of cultural competence. The frame the superintendents created was to move from the more traditional viewpoint of tolerance for diversity to personal and institutional transformation for equity. Table 4.1 illustrates their summary of how the superintendents represented the five essential elements as transformative change, as seen with the descriptors in the right column. Conversely, they illustrated corresponding descriptors for change in the left column that represent what it looks like when one tolerates change.

Moving from the conventional perspective of tolerance for diversity to the perspective of educational leaders who intentionally seek equity was an engaging process involving a commitment of time and energy. The group met in a series of 3-hour sessions held at 6-week intervals. The superintendents considered many issues that might close gaps in equity and achievement and, ultimately, decided on three outcomes for their work:

- As educational leaders, they would view issues of cultural power to be central, not ancillary, to student success.
- As educational leaders, they would develop a protocol for changing personal and organizational paradigms for school equity and achievement.
- As educational leaders, they would renew their commitment to the moral purposes of education, which are to make a positive difference in the lives of all citizens and to show individuals how to function together in a society (Graham & Lindsey, 2002).

The superintendents immersed themselves in readings about organization change, including systems theory, organization reframing,

Table 4.1   The Five Essential Elements as Leverage Points for Change

From: **TOLERANCE FOR DIVERSITY** **Destructiveness, incapacity, and** **blindness** The focus is on *them*.	To: **TRANSFORMATION FOR EQUITY** **Precompetence, competence, and** **proficiency** The focus is on *our practices*.
Assessing one's own cultural knowledge: Demographics are viewed as a challenge.	**Assessing one's own cultural knowledge:** Demographics are used to inform policy and practice.
Valuing diversity: Tolerate, assimilate, and acculturate.	**Valuing diversity:** Esteem, respect, and adapt.
Dealing with conflict: Prevent, mitigate, and avoid.	**Dealing with conflict:** Manage, leverage, and facilitate.
Adapting to diversity: Systemwide accountability to meet changing needs of a diverse community and reduce cultural dissonance and conflict.	**Adapting to diversity:** Systemwide accountability for continuous improvement and responsiveness to community. Staff understands, operates, and perseveres on the edge of often rapid and continuous change.
Integrating cultural knowledge: Information contributed or added to existing policies, procedures, and practices.	**Integrating cultural knowledge:** Information integrated into system, provoking significant changes to policies, procedures, and practices.

and transformational leadership. They read and discussed current articles on standards-based accountability. They examined and discussed student achievement data in each of their districts and posed questions to one another about how the district might be contributing to poor student performance. They concluded their study by constructing a comprehensive policy statement for equity, *Transforming Systems for Cultural Proficiency: Changing Personal and Organizational Paradigms for School Equity and Achievement* (Graham & Lindsey, 2002).

The central part of their policy statement involved arranging the cultural proficiency continuum into its two prominent components: the three points on the left side of the continuum—destructiveness, incapacity, and blindness—which focus on the behaviors of others, and the three points on the right side of the continuum—precompetence, competence, and proficiency—which focus on the behaviors of educators.

We selected this example of collaboration to demonstrate the bold steps these superintendents took in identifying initiatives for closing the achievement gap between students in their school districts. The shift in thinking that occurred among these superintendents was to examine school leadership practices. Sam Brewer, principal at Pine Hills High School, kept this shift in thinking in mind as he and Dr. Stephanie Barnes, the school improvement coach, began to work with the school leadership team to identify obstacles to student achievement at the high school.

■ Pine Hills High School's Leadership Approach to Cultural Proficiency

Culturally competent leaders are intentional in their own learning. Dr. Campbell realized this when she told the principals that she expected an analysis of the obstacles that seemed to be getting in the way of the academic and social success of each subgroup of students. Sam Brewer, the principal at Pine Hills High School, had been working with his School Leadership Team to develop their capacity in working with the concepts of cultural proficiency. Dr. Stephanie Barnes, the school improvement coach, and five teachers comprised the School Leadership Team. The teachers were Rob Moore, Joel Peters, Jack Thompson, Janice Thompson, and Maxine Parks.

Sam Brewer had taken to heart the notion that a culturally precompetent leader is aware of what he does not know and that he is willing and ready to learn. He and members of the School Leadership Team had committed considerable time to studying the guiding principles and the cultural proficiency continuum. They were now ready to use the five essential elements of cultural competence as standards and indicators for their planning. Sam distributed copies of the set of tables that comprised the *Superintendents' Collaborative for School Equity and Achievement.* He indicated that the tables represented each of the essential elements described as standards for culturally competent leadership.

■ Essential Elements as Standards for Leadership Behavior and School Policy

Tables 4.1 through 4.7 represent leadership behaviors for each of the essential elements of cultural competence. You will read how the School Leadership Team at Pine Hills High School chose to use the information in the tables. The information in the tables represents leadership actions taken in schools and provides you with clear choices to guide or assess decision making.

Sam Brewer:	As our school's leadership team, it is going to be our responsibility to do the initial planning to move our school in the direction of cultural proficiency.
Rob Moore:	I don't argue with the direction, but I am not certain how you intend that to occur? The guiding principles and the continuum information were interesting and helpful, but where do we go from here?
Maxine Parks:	Yeah, based on my understanding of the continuum, I can see the big picture, but I, too, can't see how we go about doing it. I know it has to do with the set of five standards, or essential elements.
Stephanie Barnes:	Precisely! Let me begin by sharing with you the format for our planning. From there, I will review with you the five elements as leadership standards for our work. (Stephanie distributes a one-page handout in chart form.) It is necessary for us to take what Dr. Campbell is calling bold steps, as represented in this handout:

Bold Steps Toward Cultural Proficiency

- What would cultural proficiency look like at your school?
- What are chief challenges you face in putting some of these into action at your school site?
- In light of the team's understanding of cultural proficiency, what are our values and beliefs as a team?
- Based on our values and beliefs, what three bold steps are we able to take as a team that would embrace the values of cultural proficiency at our school sites/district?
- What conditions for success will put these three bold steps in place?

Rob:	So, how would you like to proceed?
Sam:	I would like for us to do as we did at the district leadership team meeting, which is to have each of us respond individually to these statements and, then, to discuss and synthesize our thinking.

Maxine:	Well, this sure looks compelling! How do we get there?
Stephanie (laughing):	Yes, it is compelling, and before we get to this planning piece, successfully using it will require us to examine both our own motivation and the underlying assumptions of why we do the things we do.
Joe Peters:	What do you mean by, "Why we do the things we do?"
Sam:	Remember, the opportunity is for us to adapt our practices in such a way that our students have greater success, both academically and socially. In doing that, each of us will have to examine our assumptions about our students, about the curriculum we select, about the manner in which we teach, and how we interact with our community.
Janice Thompson:	Ahhhh. I am beginning to see what "inside-out" learning means.
Rob:	Yeah, me too! Now I clearly see that my learning is about my underlying assumptions, and our learning is about our practices.

We invite you to review the assumptions for each point of the continuum that you identified in Chapter 3. Reviewing those assumptions will serve you in two ways. First, in reflecting on your assumptions and reading the tables and text in this chapter, you will better understand the behaviors along the continuum and have an even deeper appreciation for how our decisions as school leaders affect students. Second, you now know if your assumptions are consistent with the standards embodied in the five essential elements of cultural competence. You can be intentional in integrating the essential elements into your professional practice.

Now that you have reviewed the information in Table 4.1, we invite you to reflect on your planning. Take a few minutes and reflect on the assumptions you listed in Chapter 3. Consider what planning for cultural proficiency means for you and your school. Use the prompts below to describe the bold steps you are willing to take for you and your school to be culturally proficient. After completing your responses, please read Tables 4.2 through 4.6, which describe the five essential elements that serve as standards for culturally competent leadership.

■ Reflective Activity: Bold Steps Toward Cultural Proficiency

What would cultural proficiency look like at your school?

_____

_____

_____

_____

_____

What are chief challenges you face in putting some of these into action at your site or district or both?

_____

_____

_____

_____

_____

In light of your school team's understanding of cultural proficiency, what are your team's values and beliefs?

_____

_____

_____

_____

_____

Based on your team's values and beliefs, what three bold steps are you able to take as a team that will embrace the values of cultural proficiency at your school site or district or both?

_____

_____

_____

_____

_____

_____

What conditions for success are necessary to put these three bold steps in place?

_____

_____

_____

_____

■ Making Sense of the Elements, Standards, and Behavior

Members of the Pine Hills High School leadership team began to study each of the essential elements, expressed as standards, and how each represented the shift from a tolerance for diversity to a transformation for equity perspective. Listen to the members of the team as they begin to read the five standards as essential elements of cultural competence and use the tables for assessing their behaviors and school practices:

Stephanie: Please keep in mind that these five standards for culturally competent leadership comprise one of the tools of cultural proficiency.

Joel: You know, I do understand that each of the essential elements serves as leadership standards for planning, but it would sure be helpful to have some greater in-depth information about them. I, for one, am fed up with that all of that theory malarkey. I want concrete examples!

Janice: Stephanie, you know what the standards and elements look like in practice. Is that what these tables are supposed to do for us?

Stephanie: Yes, I think it best if we take a concerted look at each of the essential elements. They will be helpful as we proceed with our work.

Sam: Good point! I think members of the team will find this information provocative, on one hand, and highly informative, on the other. You will see some of our current practices cast in a negative light. I encourage you to keep an open mind, to read the standards carefully, and to examine the practices on the right-hand side of each table.

In Table 4.2, the activity of assessing culture is represented in the two phases of the cultural competence continuum. Take a few minutes and read Tables 4.2 through 4.6 carefully. First, read the standard, and be certain you understand the culturally competent leadership behavior described. Then, read the contrasting behaviors represented in each of the tables. In each case, the descriptions in the left column are of behaviors that focus outward on others as being the problem, whereas the behaviors in the right column focus on changing personal practice. Personal leadership involves working with others to achieve a goal or purpose. Educational leaders who work with colleagues on issues related to teaching and learning are, in fact, focusing their attention on personal practice. Administrators' practice involves those actions that support teachers' acquiring the knowledge and skills they need to be successful with their students. As you read each of the standards and tables, notice what administrators and teachers would need to do to focus on their respective educational practices.

Standard 1—Assesses Culture: Claim Your Differences

A school leader promotes the success of all students by facilitating an examination of one's own culture, the effect it may have on others in the school, and learning about the cultures that comprise the community in which the school resides. School leaders

- Recognize how their culture affects others.
- Describe their own culture and cultural norms of their organization.
- Understand how the culture of their schools affects those with different cultures.

This standard introduces the notion of the inside-out approach to change. The focus is within, whether it is the administrator, the

Table 4.2 Leadership Behaviors for Assessing One's Own Culture

From: **TOLERANCE FOR DIVERSITY** **Destructiveness, incapacity, and** **blindness** The focus is on *them*.	To: **TRANSFORMATION FOR EQUITY** **Precompetence, competence, and** **proficiency** The focus is on *our practices*.
When assessing one's and the school's culture, the leader views changing demographics as a challenge. The leader	**When assessing one's own and the school's culture, the leader studies demographics to inform policy and practice. The leader**
upholds practices that present changing demographics to be barriers/obstacles to current educational practice, organization, funding, governance, systemwide effectiveness, and accountability.	analyzes demographic data to assess their cultural knowledge and to examine the mismatch between the intent of the system and the outcomes for clients served.
implements policies that maintain that students, their families, languages, class, race/ethnicity, and neighborhoods are academic, social, and economic deficits and in need of intervention and remediation.	implements policies in which students, their families, languages, race/ethnicity, and neighborhoods are used as resources to enhance the way the school provides resources to ensure high expectations and the attainment of rigorous standards for all.
presents reform as driven by external audits, compliance reviews, litigation, or threat of sanctions from funding or oversight agencies (state departments of education, U.S. Department of Education, Office of Civil Rights, U.S. Department of Justice, American Civil Liberties Union, etc.)	initiates transformative change driven by higher moral purpose—to make a democracy possible, to make a positive difference in the lives of students, and to teach individuals how they can function effectively and together in a diverse society.

counselor, the teacher, the grade level, the department, the school, or the district. The culturally proficient leader is introspective and is interested to know the effect that his or her culture has on others. The culturally proficient leader studies the culture of the school and its grade levels or departments. Leaders use the insights gained from personal introspection and examination of the school culture to help others acclimatize to the school and for leaders and the school to make changes that invite others to become part of an ever-evolving school organization.

Table 4.2 represents the two phases of the cultural proficiency continuum. The leader behaviors in the left column portray behaviors that tolerate diversity and changing demographics. Leadership behaviors in the right column are those demonstrated when the examination of professional practices leads to professional and personal transformation.

Maxine: Hmmm, this first one is interesting. Where did it come from?

Sam: They were developed a couple of years ago by a group of superintendents in the Los Angeles area who decided they wanted to find ways to close the achievement gap.

Janice: Wow, this first table [Table 4.2] is busy!

Maxine: Yeah, it sure is.

Sam: Well, what do you see?

Janice: Several things! First, as you can see, one's leadership skills become more appropriate as you move from the left column to the right column.

Joel: This could be very uncomfortable for some people!

Rob: What do you mean?

Joel: What I mean is, it is very possible I could find a decision or attitude I have that appears negative on this continuum.

Sam: That is the beauty of this table. If you find a behavior or attitude that reflects a decision or belief of yours, you can see other choices you have. Remember, cultural competence is about being intentional with one's behavior.

Maxine: That's helpful!

Stephanie: Good, because this deepens our understanding of the element.

[Janice and Joel nod in agreement.]

Rob: You know, Sam, as I continue to look at this table, I see a lot of our behaviors at this school not being what I want for us!

Jack: Such as?

Rob: Well, I have been here for 22 years, and in that time, we
            have had a major demographic shift in our student
            population. I am willing to bet that some of these illus-
            trations about the school not changing do apply to us.
            Also, our increased reliance on discipline. Whooee, this
            is going to be interesting!

Maxine: Yes, but the redeeming feature is that we have illustra-
            tions for more appropriate choices. It is really helpful to
            see concrete illustrations. As I look at the remaining
            four tables, I can readily see how they will be helpful as
            we continue our planning.

Stephanie: Let's take a look at the content in the next four
            standards.

Standard 2—Values Diversity: Name the Differences

A school leader welcomes diversity into the school by developing a community of learning within the school and with parents
and other interested members of the school community. The school
leader

- States that tolerance and respect are initial steps on the way to
  valuing diversity.
- Celebrates and encourages the presence of a variety of people
  in all activities to maximize perspective and experiences.
- Recognizes differences as diversity rather than as inappropriate responses to the school community.
- Accepts that each culture finds some values and behaviors
  more important than others do.

School administrators and other school leaders have the moral
responsibility to set a positive tone for valuing diversity in schools.
For too long, we have turned a blind eye to the different experiences
students have in our schools. One of the constructive features of the
accountability movement is that we now have the opportunity to
examine subgroup data. Access to data is one of the great revolutions of the past decade that has affected virtually all schools. We
can readily gather data and array them by demographic groupings,
to learn how academically and socially successful are our students.

However, the data alone are not liberating. It is the perspective that we take to the data that permits us to be effective in working cross-culturally. This becomes the moral responsibility of school leaders, whether administrators or teachers. Fullan (2003) sets forth the following criteria that address the moral purpose of schools:

- All students and teachers benefit in terms of identified desirable goals.
- The gap between high and low performers becomes less as the bar for all is raised.
- Ever-deeper educational goals are pursued.
- The culture of the school becomes so transformed that continuous improvement relative to the previous three components becomes built-in (p. 31).

In Table 4.3, you will see the contrasting phases of valuing diversity along the cultural competence continuum. Note how the behaviors in the left column serve to abdicate our responsibility, whereas the behaviors in the right column are proactive in ways that cause us to examine our educational practices.

Standard 3—Manages the Dynamics of Difference: Frame the Conflicts Caused by Differences

A school leader recognizes that conflict is a natural and normal part of life and learns to manage conflict to the best interest of all involved. The school leader

- Learns and uses effective strategies for resolving conflict, particularly among people whose cultural backgrounds and values differ.
- Understands the effect that historic distrust has on present-day interactions.
- Realizes that one may misjudge others' actions based on learned expectations.

School administrators and other school leaders can create a constructive and instructive environment for managing conflict. Conflict is natural and normal in human relationships and within any organization, even in so-called homogeneous communities. Schools, by their very nature, are complex organizations composed of different educator roles, parents with whom to relate, political interactions with regulatory agencies, and varied community

Table 4.3   Leadership Behaviors for Valuing Diversity

From: **TOLERANCE FOR DIVERSITY** Destructiveness, incapacity, and blindness The focus is on *them*.	To: **TRANSFORMATION FOR EQUITY** Precompetence, competence, and proficiency The focus is on *our practices*.
When the leader encounters cultures different from hers, her approach to is to tolerate, assimilate, and acculturate. The leader	**When encountering cultures different from his, the leader's approach to diversity is to value, esteem, respect, and adapt. The leader**
states that others are the products of an educational, socioeconomic, or cultural deficit, and she focuses the school system in helping them to assimilate, while she leads the effort to maintain the cultural/educational status quo.	sponsors an inside-out systemic approach that leads the system, and individuals within it, to examine how well student/community needs are being met, and then adapts so multiple voices are heard and integrated into the formulation of policy and practice.
employs a standards-based accountability system that discounts knowledge from nondominant groups, that excludes some learning and communication styles, and that may be have punitive effects on underperforming students.	uses standards to ensure high expectations for all, differentiated instruction, multiple assessment, and resources to ensure success of underperforming students.
uses professional development training to focus on understanding others and improving communication with them.	sponsors professional development training that focuses on understanding of self and how to identify and remove existing barriers to equity and education.

constituent groups. Then, when we add racial, ethnic, gender, social class, religious, and sexual orientation diversity issues, we have real schools in real communities. In these diverse settings, managing the dynamics of difference is about how conflict can deepen understanding among cultural groups. An educational leader who values diversity uses the current situation to provide others with the information and skills that inform one another of our respective histories, languages, lifestyles, and worldviews (Lindsey et al., 2003; Nuri Robins et al., 2002).

Table 4.4 represents the behaviors of managing the dynamics of difference in the two phases of the cultural competence continuum. Culturally proficient behaviors are representative of the personal transformation that occurs when one assumes responsibility for one's behavior.

Table 4.4 Leadership Behaviors for Managing the Dynamics of Difference

From: **TOLERANCE FOR DIVERSITY** **Destructiveness, incapacity, and blindness** The focus is on *them*.	To: **TRANSFORMATION FOR EQUITY** **Precompetence, competence, and proficiency** The focus is on *our practices*.
When dealing with conflict that arises from cross-cultural contact, the leader's response is to prevent, mitigate, and avoid. The leader	**When dealing with conflict that arises from cross-cultural contact, the leader's response is to manage, leverage, and facilitate. The leader**
avoids dissonant, controversial topics and issues.	facilitates, challenges, and provokes positive conflict and discussion about difficult topics and issues.
seeks commonalities through early agreement and consensus to unite divided/diverse groups. Difference is viewed as threatening, risky, and divisive.	seeks difference over commonality by helping the group to learn from dissonance and to forge new, more complex agreements and capabilities that transform the organization to be able to respond to multiple perspectives and voices.
expresses the assumption that the system is fair for everyone if the rules are followed. He calls attention to the good intentions of individuals in the system. He assumes those who are different are judged and treated fairly (race, gender, sexual orientation, socioeconomic class, religion, age, etc.)	acknowledges historical inequity for some groups. She openly recognizes one's own agentry as a beneficiary of race, gender, orientation, class, religion, or age privilege.
states that populations not expressing conflict do not need training or development for cultural proficiency.	states that homogeneous populations need training and development for cultural proficiency to ensure that silence or passivity do not mask repressed conflict.
recruits, hires, and promotes individuals who are like-minded.	recruits, hires, and promotes people who think and act differently from those already in the system.

Standard 4—Institutionalize
Cultural Knowledge: Teach About Differences

A school leader provides opportunities for school and community colleagues to use information about the school and community cultures in ways that honor and challenge continuous learning. The school leader

- Incorporates cultural knowledge into the mainstream of the organization.
- Teaches the origins of stereotypes and prejudices.
- Integrates into school systems information and skills that enable all to interact effectively in a variety of intercultural situations.

Educational leaders, administrators, counselors, or teachers are the managers of cultural knowledge. It is within their domain of power to decide what is to be included. The key components of institutionalizing cultural knowledge are learning about your own culture and the culture of your own school (or grade level or department) and learning how each group experiences the school (Nuri Robins et al., 2002). Whether the current initiative is an increasingly diverse faculty or it is examining the disaggregated data of student achievement, culturally proficient leaders sponsor professional development that demonstrates a commitment to life-long learning. The culturally proficient leader works hard not to dichotomize learning. He or she infuses the learning of knowledge and skills about technology, standards, and curriculum with an ever-deeper understanding of how people learn and transmit their cultural values. Chapter 7 presents a template for leading in a culture of transformative change.

Table 4.5 is more detailed than the other tables in this chapter. The categories in this table represent prominent leadership actions to institutionalize cultural knowledge—curriculum and instruction, assessment, training and professional development, and parent communication/community outreach. As with the previous examples, the behaviors in the left column represent additive actions that have the effect of tolerance. In contrast, the behaviors in the right column represent personal leadership and organizational transformation.

Table 4.5   Leadership Behaviors for Institutionalizing Cultural Knowledge

From: **TOLERANCE FOR DIVERSITY** **Destructiveness, incapacity, and blindness** The focus is on *them*.	To: **TRANSFORMATION FOR EQUITY** **Precompetence, competence, and proficiency** The focus is on *our practices*.
Information is added to existing policies, procedures, and practices.	**Information is integrated into the system, provoking significant changes to policies, procedures, and practices.**
A. Curriculum and instruction: The leader adds to current practice, in that he or she	**A. Curriculum and instruction: The leader fosters change in the system, in that he or she**
employs the use of rigorous standards to drive curriculum. Alternate curriculum/curricular paths or remedial interventions are provided for underperforming students.	uses a rigorous standards-driven curriculum in which teachers use scaffolding and research-based strategies to ensure all student progress toward standards.
adds multicultural content, activities, and resources to the curriculum and/or sponsors school programs to acknowledge the contributions of racial, ethnic, and cultural groups.	integrates multiple perspectives about topics, issues, themes, and events into the curriculum. Textbooks and other resources accurately and positively portray cultural/ethnic/racial/gender groups.
schedules multicultural/diversity programs for students and/or staff that focus on understanding others, conflict resolution, behavior management tolerance, and character education.	focuses multicultural/diversity programs for students and staff on one's own cultural proficiency to help the organization identify and remove barriers to achievement for all students.
B. Assessment: The leader adds to current practice, in that the leader	**B. Assessment: The leader fosters change in the system, in that the leader**
uses only assessment procedures and methods that are tightly controlled by nationally normed tests.	uses school/classroom assessment procedures that are openly shared, flexible, and do not dominate the curriculum.
schedules instructional time to be spent on test-prep for tests that have high-stakes consequences for some students.	ensures that students have multiple, varied opportunities to demonstrate progress. Assessment strategies support

students in demonstrating what they know and guide them to improve and expand their learning.

requires teachers to provide alternate intervention/remediation, often in pullout programs, for students not making progress toward standards.

disaggregates data and frequently uses formative assessments with teachers to plan, monitor, and adjust instruction and to provide specific feedback about progress toward clear learning targets that support grade level content standards.

confines primary users of assessment to teachers and school/district staff.

involves students and parents in assessing student achievement.

uses rubrics to ensure consistent, fair assessment of student work.

shares and uses rubrics as instructional tools to articulate learning targets and standards to all.

has special-needs students waived out of many schoolwide assessments.

makes accommodations to maximize success for special-needs students.

C. Training and professional development: The leader adds to current practice, in that he or she

C. Training and professional development: The leader fosters change in the system, in that he or she

sponsors professional development that is compliance driven. Participation is often mandatory.

sponsors professional development that is driven by the desire to transform the self, first, to develop the organization's cultural proficiency.

promotes multicultural education designed to heighten feelings of inclusion for minority students, to help all students understand each other better, and to reduce conflict and violence on school campuses. Those closest to the students (teachers and support staff) are the primary audience for multicultural education/diversity training.

uses long-term, systemwide equity-based diversity training to identify and remove barriers to achievement that requires all staff and stakeholders to be trained via processes that provoke dialogue, challenge assumptions, and catalyze change for individuals and the organization. Those responsible for facilitating changes at all levels of the system are the primary audience for training.

designs and implements professional development outcomes that result in the addition of multicultural units to the curriculum, the addition of multicultural artifacts on display in

designs and implements training outcomes to result in the creation of curriculum in which students value other cultural groups. Individual and organizational changes result

(Continued)

Table 4.5 (Continued)

classrooms and the school, and the addition of multicultural celebrations and assemblies to the extracurricular program.	in closing the gaps in achievement, performance, and success experienced disproportionately by members of some student groups.
D. Parent communication/ community outreach: The leader adds to current practice, in that he or she	**D. Parent communication/ community outreach: The leader fosters change in the system, in that he or she**
encourages parents to share cultural information, artifacts, and traditions to enrich school programs.	involves parents from multiple cultural groups as active collaborators in school/district decision making. The school communicates in the language of the parents/community, providing interpreters, child care, food, transportation, etc. Alternate meeting times and locations meet the needs of the community. Meeting agendas address community issues and concerns.
solicits parents to participate on school advisory committees, especially those committees that address concerns of specific cultural groups.	involves parents as partners in important decisions that affect their children's education.
seeks information for educators and staff that promotes understanding about community cultures via multiple information resources and school/district orientations and training sessions.	has all staff interact with families at school events and in local community settings to gain authentic information and understanding about community cultures.

Standard 5—Adapts to Diversity:
Change to Make a Difference

A school leader promotes continuous learning with his or her school and community colleagues to mitigate issues arising from differences in experiences and perspectives. The school leader

- Changes the current way of doing things to acknowledge the differences that are present in the staff, clients, and community.
- Develops skills for intercultural communication.
- Institutionalizes cultural interventions for conflicts and confusion caused by the dynamics of difference.

To adapt to diversity is first to recognize that everyone changes and that change is ongoing. Faculties change as teachers, counselors, and administrators leave and new people take their places. Communities change as people leave for new lives elsewhere and new families take their places. Often, these changes include the cultural compositions of schools. We expect school leaders, irrespective of the demographic profile of the school, to ensure the success of students of all cultural groups and from all parts of the community. As new groups of people move into the community or as gaps in students' success are identified, the educational leaders are responsible for the initial learning. They have the responsibility to learn about the histories, languages, lifestyles, and worldviews of the people who are new to the school.

This initial learning is fundamental to adaptation. Adapting to diversity is the embodiment of change as a process in which school leaders have made a personal and institutional commitment to that process. The culturally proficient leader uses his or her knowledge about the new members of the community, in combination with skills in managing the dynamics of difference, to educate the staff. It is the leader's responsibility to impart the new knowledge and skills in such a way that the faculty will learn the respective histories, languages, lifestyles, and worldviews of the changing community.

Table 4.6 represents the behavior of adapting to diversity at the two phases of the cultural competence continuum. As in the previous tables, the behaviors in the left column describe tolerating diversity, and the behaviors in the right column describe initiatives leaders take when committing to serving the needs of the total community.

The five essential elements of cultural competence serve as standards by which leaders and school leadership teams can guide their work. The School Leadership Team at Pine Hills High School has completed its initial review of the five tables. Let's listen to their conversation:

Stephanie: Well, what do you think?

[There are several minutes of silence. Then, Rob speaks.]

Rob: I am a little speechless, a little angry, a little hopeful—a lot confused!

Sam: It is not easy, is it?

Janice: I won't try to speak for Rob, but this is intimidating. I found our examination of the guiding principles to be challenging. For me, the continuum was eye-opening. But, this is a lot!

Table 4.6   Leadership Behaviors for Adapting to Diversity

From: **TOLERANCE FOR DIVERSITY** **Destructiveness, incapacity, and blindness** The focus is on *them*.	To: **TRANSFORMATION FOR EQUITY** **Precompetence, competence, and proficiency** The focus is on *our practices*.
Leaders respond to systemwide accountability and to meet the changing needs of a diverse community and to reduce cultural dissonance and conflict. As the leader, he or she	**Leaders use systemwide accountability for continuous improvement and responsiveness to community. Staff understands, operates, and perseveres on the edge of often rapid and continuous change. As the leader, he or she**
develops and uses multiple programs to meet multiple goals. System monitors resource allocation and accountability to funding source.	integrates important themes, programs, and goals. Resources are combined and allocated equitably to students and communities most in need.
invests in recruiting and hiring new staff that is competent, committed, and caring.	invests, at the district level, in capacity building of staff that is competent, committed, and caring.
has a laser-like focus on high expectations and achievement and an orientation for timely intervention and remediation for students not making progress.	has a laser-like focus on high expectations and achievement and an orientation for prevention of student learning gaps.
holds teachers accountable for high standards for all students and high-quality instruction based on standards.	holds teachers, administrator, staff, parents, and students accountable for high standards and quality instruction. Stakeholders ensure that standards-based instruction and accountability for test scores do not result in diminished educational quality or negative educational consequences for any student/student groups.

Stephanie: What do you mean, "a lot"?

Janice: Well, as someone said earlier, I find a lot of my and the school's behaviors on the left side of these tables. I am not sure I agree in all cases.

Sam: Well, let's eat this elephant one bite at a time.

Joel: Yes, that is a good idea. Like Rob and Janice, I had the same initial reaction to the tables. But, as I continue to look at them, the information on the right side of the tables does seem to make sense.

Maxine: I agree. What is interesting to me is how these examples really make our earlier discussions of the guiding principles come alive for me.

Stephanie: Are you ready to move forward?

[All nod in agreement, although seemingly some appear to be feeling dissonant.]

Stephanie: To assist us in this planning, Dr. Campbell has devised a template for strategic planning for cultural competence to help us in doing this work. It is titled "Template— Strategic Planning for Cultural Competence."

Template for Strategic Planning

Educators motivated to become culturally proficient do so with moral intent, often in the face of resistance within their schools and districts. Whether you undertake this journey to follow your own values and beliefs or if you are working with a team, strategic planning is critical. Table 4.7 is for you to use in combination with Tables 4.1 through 4.6.

Tables 4.1 through 4.6 provide you and your colleagues with detailed examples of culturally competent behaviors in the columns on the right in each chart. The columns on the left in each table provide you with illustrations of behaviors that, if you are using them, you will want to reconsider their use. The template in Table 4.7 provides a framework for recording your selected leadership actions, the person(s) responsible for the actions, and the agreed-upon timeline.

Again, we invite you to review the assumptions for each point on the continuum that you identified in Chapter 3. Reviewing those assumptions will serve you in two ways. First, in reflecting on your assumptions and reading the tables and text in this chapter, you better understand the behaviors along the continuum and have an even deeper appreciation for how our decisions as school leaders affect students. Second, you now know if your assumptions

Table 4.7   Template: Strategic Planning for Cultural Competence

Essential element	What leadership action is to be taken?	Who will do it?	By when?
Assessing cultural knowledge			
Valuing diversity			
Managing the dynamics of difference			
Institutionalizing cultural knowledge			
Curriculum and instruction			
Assessment			
Training and professional development			
Parent and community outreach			
Adapting to diversity			

are consistent with the standards embodied in the five essential elements of cultural competence. Now you can be intentional in integrating the essential elements into your professional practice.

5

Overcoming Self-Imposed Barriers to Moral Leadership

Do we have the will to educate all children?

—Asa Hilliard (1991, p. 31)

The Maple View Elementary School leadership team members have decided it is time to begin the deeper work of cultural proficiency and have invited Dr. Campbell to help them move to the next level. It has been a couple of weeks since Dr. Campbell initiated this process, so she is very interested to find out how they are individually involved with creating a school culture that is committed to educating all children. She recognizes that this venture is not without risk, but it is a worthwhile risk if the Maple View School District is to be serious about educating all children and youth.

Dr. Campbell offered opening comments to the leadership team meeting: "Our state legislature enacted the Public School Accountability Act in 1999. How many of you were teachers, counselors, or administrators before that time?" Most of the participants raised their

---

AUTHORS' NOTE: This chapter is adapted from Lindsey (2001).

hands in acknowledgment. She noted that it was a largely veteran force, but there were a couple who were new to education.

She continued, "How many began your education careers that year or later?" Only two people raised their hands. "As a school district, we have been analyzing disaggregated data as required by the Public School Accountability Act." Most nodded their heads, indicating their agreement with her. Dr. Campbell was aware that for many administrators and teachers, learning how to use student data was a new and often time-consuming process. In many schools, there had been resistance to the new accountability measures. "Of those of you who raised your hands, how many were aware of the disparities that the disaggregated data have revealed?" Along with the participants, Barbara raised her hand. She looked across the group and asked, "What does that say about us? We have been aware of these disparities for years but waited for the state legislature to get us moving!"

Barbara and the leadership team came face to face with the reality of the quote, "Do we have the will to educate all children?" Asa Hilliard (1991) posed this question to our profession more than 10 years ago. However, we continue to struggle to answer it. The question invokes a sense of moral purpose or responsibility. The question carries with it a veiled accusation—that we have not been educating all children and, indeed, maybe we do not have the will to do so.

The achievement gap is one of the worst secrets in the education community. It is, too often, the undiscussable issue that educators grudgingly have acknowledged but about which we have not had the courage to explore in meaningful ways. The current accountability movement provides the opportunity to examine disaggregated student achievement data by subgroups. This has shed light on facts that we educators have hidden in aggregated student results. This illumination is revealing the genuine disparities and inequities that are accepted by educators as "the way things are" or "We're doing pretty well, considering . . ." Long overdue in this ongoing discussion is admitting that there is an achievement gap. Educators are beginning to concede the situation is an ethical and moral imperative (Fullan, 1991, 2003; Sergiovanni, 1992). In truth, we have been complicit in the undereducation, if not the noneducation, of our children and youth from low-socioeconomic, Native American, African American, Latino, English-learning, and special education groups.

In Chapter 3, we described how culturally precompetent and culturally competent educators use the moral authority of their school leadership positions to successfully confront issues of oppression. We recognize that the word *oppression* is emotive for some people, and readers may react negatively to our use of this word to describe educational policies and practices. However, the disparities that are maintained in our educational system are, indeed, oppressive and serve to maintain the position, power, and privilege of the dominant group. Most assuredly, the term oppression is an appropriate descriptor for the fact that issues of undereducation continue to exist generation after generation.

It is our experience that many educators are stuck in trying to combat the continuing effects of "-isms"—racism, ethnocentrism, sexism, heterosexism, and ableism. The roadblock that people must circumvent often begins with what we refer to as "doing their own work." First, a person must understand his or her own feelings about uncomfortable information. Second, the individual must take actions that are in the best interest of the students. This "feeling-to-action" connection either impedes or facilitates action.

■ Reflective Activity

When you hear or use words such as *racism*, *ethnocentrism*, or *sexism*, what are the thoughts that come to mind?

_____

_____

_____

_____

_____

_____

What feelings do the "-isms" words generate in you?

_____

_____

_____

_____

_____

_____

Returning to Maple View Elementary School, we find members of the school leadership team continuing to struggle. Joan Stephens and Connie Barkley were commiserating about their most recent cultural proficiency session. Joan was struggling with her deep, emotional reactions to the session. She knew that Connie had sponsored the session and felt that she could share with Connie some of her concerns and questions:

Joan:	Connie, you know from the very beginning, way back when Dr. Campbell first started talking about cultural proficiency, that I have been in full support of this effort. But, after our session yesterday, something is really bothering me.
Connie:	What is it, Joan? How can I help you?
Joan:	Well, I guess mostly by just listening.
Connie:	Is it fair to ask "hard" questions?
Joan:	Oh, that's scary. What do you mean?
Connie:	Well, maybe I am anticipating your comments, but I am struck by your using the phrase about "being in full support of this cultural proficiency effort." And then you attached the notorious "but." Is that where you want to begin?
Joan (somewhat deflated):	Well, yeah. I am stunned by how quickly you went to the heart of the matter. Connie, I listened to the speaker, I read the book, I engaged in the activities, but I cannot escape feeling blamed.
Connie:	It would be helpful for me to describe what you mean by "feeling blamed."
Joan:	Arrrgggghh! Sometimes I feel angry; other times I feel guilty. However, I know those feelings are not productive, so I just sit on them.
Connie:	No you don't Joan. You internalize them to anger, guilt, or frustration. I am never sure which it is.
Joan:	What do you mean?
Connie:	Joan, we have been friends and colleagues for several years, and I think I know a little about you as a person. Frankly, Joan, you seem to want the Cliffs Notes

version of cultural proficiency. I think Dr. Campbell has really tried to help us see that cultural proficiency isn't our latest project; it's about how we view our work and our interactions with our students. Our values and beliefs are most evident in the assumptions we have about our students.

Joan: Connie, I think I understand that. But, what do you mean about my wanting the "Cliffs Notes version of cultural proficiency"?

Connie: Remember what our facilitator said yesterday: We must understand systems of oppression and their impact. For example, think about racism and its effects on people at both a personal and institutional level.

Joan: Okay?

Connie: Racism negatively impacts both the victims and the perpetrators and interjects destructive energy into the system—like the school or a classroom. By understanding this double-edged impact, we are more able to see and feel the effects of oppression and work to combat it. We are more prepared to ask ourselves hard questions about our own assumptions and their effects. It's not easy to question our intentions and the intentions that are unwittingly institutionalized in our organizations. And yet, this is the only way we can change things.

Joan: Then, why do I feel this way?

Connie: Your feelings are natural and normal, Joan, and a courageous question you might ask is: "What are you willing to do, and how are you willing to change to create the best learning environment for all students at this school?" Joan, we can't be the observers in this change process. We are the leaders. Our feelings can be indications of being on the verge of deeper and more powerful learning.

Joan: You make it sound like resistance or denial.

Connie: Just imagine, Joan, if you have the feelings you are describing, what it is like for the students who are not succeeding at this school? And, you're a parent, Joan. Think about how your students' parents must feel when they don't see value added for their children being in our schools. They also may feel angry, guilty, and frustrated by the circumstances they are caught up in.

This conversation between Joan and Connie illustrates the authors' belief and experience that too often, educators stand on the sidelines, observing oppression and its disastrous results rather than becoming personally involved with them. As Dr. Campbell found out from her questions to her educator colleagues, we have known of the achievement gap for decades and as a profession have done alarmingly little about it. As educational leaders, the questions for us are as follows:

- How did we arrive at these disparities in our schools?
- How do the forces of entitlement and privilege affect our profession?
- What are these feelings of anger and guilt, and why do I have them?
- What are our responsibilities as school leaders?

■ Reflective Activity

What educational disparities for students do you see in your school or district?

_____

_____

_____

_____

_____

Please describe your reactions to the disparities in your school.

_____

_____

_____

_____

_____

_____

Entitlement and Privilege as Education History

At the dawn of the 20th century, a comprehensive education was an opportunity not available to most citizens. In one century, our country has progressed from offering a comprehensive public education to a small portion of the population to making public education available to most people. In the early 21st century, the promise and the possibility still exist, but the promise is unfulfilled. Well-informed educational leaders may be the linchpins of our democracy, serving our citizens in ways not envisioned by our counterparts a century ago.

During the past century, as this country matured, greater access to a comprehensive public education resulted from economic and legal pressures. The economic growth of the country demanded an increasingly better-educated workforce. However, women and people of color had to rely on judicial and legislative actions to participate fully in public education as a means for gaining entry into the economic mainstream of our country. School desegregation, Title IX, and Public Law 94-142 are examples of legislative and judicial steps used to gain access to educational opportunities.

However, access did not guarantee a quality education. It is only recently, and often due to the pressures exerted by judicial decisions and legislative actions, that schools have begun to address the needs of diverse populations. The accountability movements that are in place in federal and state initiatives expect, for the first time in our history, that all students, irrespective of their cultural backgrounds, will achieve a standards-based education. As controversial as these initiatives may be, they stand in a long line of modern educational initiatives. The most prominent of these initiatives was the _Brown v. Topeka Board of Education_ (1954) decision that led to school desegregation. Desegregation efforts since the 1960s have been preoccupied with the thorny issues of physical access to school campuses and have only recently become involved with both the input and the output of the educational process. Prekindergarten through Grade 12 schools have experienced segregation, desegregation, and integration, and they still struggle to provide an effective education to all sectors of society. Today's school leaders are in a unique position to become advocates for all children and youth to receive a comprehensive education and also to help build communities that affirm goals of academic and social success.

During the latter part of the 20th century, terms such as *diversity* and *multiculturalism* described a complex society that had always existed but was rarely acknowledged by the dominant culture. These changes are pushing us beyond unquestioned acceptance of the prevailing view of early 20th-century white male scholars who predominated in establishing the policies and practices of U.S. public education (Bohn & Sleeter, 2000; Sheets, 2000). The achievement gap is the lingering evidence of historical inequities and a persistent challenge to educational leaders.

Once people understand the concepts of entitlement and privilege, they must also have the will to make the ethical and moral choices implicit in such an understanding. One of the common denominators for all systems of oppression is that people lose rights and benefits due to discrimination against them. Privilege and entitlement occur when rights and privileges denied to one group of people accrue to others, often taken for granted in unrecognized and unacknowledged ways. For example, if you cannot vote because of your skin color and I can vote because of mine, functionally I have two votes—mine and the one denied to you. Similarly, if I have access to an enriched educational experience that involves higher thinking skills and you are stuck, year after year, in low-level drill instruction, I will be better prepared than you to perform well on any measure of academic success placed before me.

Transformational Leadership

As you read in Chapter 4, moving from being culturally precompetent to being culturally competent entails a shift in thinking. A component of this shift in thinking is to understand the concepts of entitlement and privilege and their relationship to systems of oppression. Racism and other forms of oppression exist only because the dominant group benefits from the continued practices. Culturally competent educational leaders shift their thinking and are intentional in understanding not only the negative consequences of oppression but also the benefits of those same systems.

We must become "the change we want to be" (Gandhi, 2002). Mahatma Mohandas K. Gandhi's words let us know that we are at the heart of creating the world we envision. It requires a personal transformation that leads to dismantling systems of oppression, such as racism. This necessarily involves the deconstruction of power in both personal and institutional forms. Weick (1979) holds that organization is a myth and that "most 'things' in organizations are actually relationships tied together in systematic fashion" (p. 88). In other words, we invent social organizations through our interactions with one another. Cultural destructiveness and cultural proficiency are similarly invented ways of organizing our social interactions. The choice is ours: We can continue to perpetuate historical racism and inequity, or we can lead our organizations to historical levels of effectiveness and achievement. It is all invented: A human invention is created by those within the system called "school" (Zander & Zander, 2000).

The transformational leadership behaviors described in the culturally precompetent, culturally competent, and culturally proficient environment illustrations in Chapter 4 exist within the context of our moral authority as educational leaders. To make the shift from culturally precompetent to culturally competent is to recognize the dynamics of entitlement and privilege, to recognize that our schools contribute to disparities in achievement, and to believe that educators can make choices that positively affect student success. Cultural competence requires a leadership perspective that involves an inside-out approach to personal and organizational change. Culturally proficient leaders redefine education in a democracy to be inclusive. These leaders focus on inequity and equity, regardless of who is benefiting from the current status. They focus on confronting and changing one's own behavior to learning from and about new groups in the community, rather than how to change and assimilate members of target groups. Culturally proficient leaders expect criticism from influential people, and they operate in school districts by remaining centered on the moral value in our work as educators.

Coming to grips with privilege and entitlement is not without risk. The risk comes in questioning the process of public schooling and the institutional structures, policies, and practices that shape the learning processes in schools. Understanding privilege and entitlement and questioning the systems that support them require countering the legacy of history that has provided us with an educational system that is designed to educate some students and not others. Therefore, the hard question becomes: How have I benefited from the privilege and entitlement accorded to me as a result of my skin color, gender, social class, sexual orientation, age, and experience? (Kovel 1984; Tatum, 1999).

■ Reflective Activity

What is entitlement or privilege?

_____

_____

_____

_____

_____

_____

How do you relate entitlement or privilege to "-ism," such as racism or sexism?

_____

_____

_____

_____

_____

_____

What are the risks involved for you as you transform your behaviors from cultural blindness to cultural precompetence?

_____

_____

_____

_____

_____

_____

Facing Entitlement: The Conundrum
of Anger, Guilt, or Confidence

Reactions to new information can often be discomforting. What was your reaction to the "hard question" in the preceding section? For many people, engaging in conversation about the topics of privilege and entitlement can generate an emotional reaction that can range from anger to guilt. However, once people acknowledge and understand their very real feelings about this new learning, along with their recognition of the very real outcomes of privilege and entitlement, they are ready to begin learning to work more effectively with students and communities that are culturally different from theirs. This level of learning is empowering in that an individual can consciously direct his or her own learning and can continue discovering ways to be effective in working in cross-cultural situations (Cross, 1989; Freire, 1970, 1999). In the following vignette, you will see how two educators at Maple View Elementary School surface their feelings about entitlement and privilege:

Joan: You know, I can take this discussion of racism and sexism, when the presenters are not so aggressive. Enough is enough!

Connie: What do you mean by aggressive?

Joan: Well, she just kept presenting information that is so very uncomfortable.

Connie: But, I do recall her asking you how you felt about the information and what your thoughts were. How is that aggressive? Do you think it would have been different for you if a white male had presented the information?

Joan: Why would you ask me if I would have reacted differently had the information on racism and sexism been presented by a white male?

Connie: Well, as I see it, the presenter was not aggressive toward you. She merely presented ideas that you appeared to find upsetting.

Joan: Upsetting? How the hell can you say that?

Connie: Look at yourself right now—you have raised your voice, and you are pointing your finger right into my chest. If that is not anger, I don't know what is!

Joan: Listen, dammit, I resent people trying to make me feel guilty for something I did not create. I am fully prepared to be accountable for my actions, but I am not going to feel guilty for what "history" or "institutions" have done to anyone!

Educators such as Joan often become upset when discussing oppression and act out forms of anger or guilt or both. Figure 5.1 represents this range of reactions. People who have the ability to listen to the information and not accept the information as anger or guilt are confident they can use the information for constructive purposes.

Figure 5.1   Continuum of Reactions to Information About Oppression

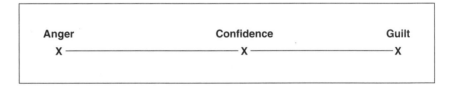

Educational leaders who choose to remain angry or guilty when dealing with facts about the disparate success of students identified in subgroup categories of race, gender, sexual orientation, social class, language acquisition, or special needs contribute to their own paralysis of inaction or inappropriate action. Figure 5.2 indicates that feelings of anger and guilt, although very different, are similarly dysfunctional for school leaders. The sense of frustration that arises from feelings of anger and guilt leads to inaction which does not benefit underachieving students. Worse, the sense of frustration can lead to actions that are counterproductive for underachieving students. However, the educational leader who moves beyond his or her initial feelings and can understand the underlying issues of oppression will be able to confront such issues with confidence. The leader's confidence is rooted in having made a moral decision to choose to use methods and materials that are effective for each group of students at the school.

Making conscious, intentional choices is a mark of an educator who strives to improve his or her practice. Typically, for teachers and counselors, practice is improved by selecting and delivering curriculum and instruction that meet the needs of each and every demographic

Figure 5.2   Functional and Dysfunctional Reactions to Issues of
Oppression

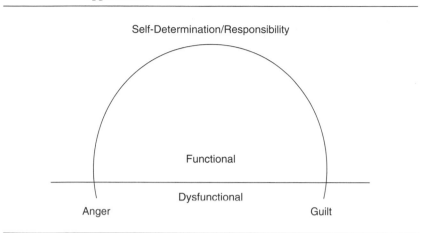

group of students. For school administrators, practice is improved through marshaling resources in support of high-quality curriculum and instruction. Members of professional organizations and unions improve practice by ensuring that their core values address service to their students. At the policy-making level, improvement of practice involves school board members and district administrators setting and implementing policy that provides for access by students from all sectors of the community. The confident person is proactive and asserts his or her needs, opinions, and views. This person also takes responsibility to facilitate others, particularly those who are silent, in understanding that their feelings may be an important avenue to new learning.

What is different about the members of these two groups of educators—those stuck in dysfunction and those who are able to move forward with confidence? It is the successful transition in a shift in thinking and disposition from cultural destructiveness, cultural incapacity, and cultural blindness to cultural precompetence and, eventually, cultural competence. The point between these two positions is what Gladwell (2000) termed the "tipping point." It is that point in time when a shift in thinking occurs. The shift in thinking occurs when the educational leader sees the behaviors of cultural destructiveness, incapacity, and blindness as inauthentic and moves to the arenas of possibility provided by culturally competent behaviors. The shift in thinking occurs when leaders recognize their stereotypic feelings and reactions and, through a process of reflection, begin to examine their practice. You can see it in their eyes; it is a moment of surprise, often expressed as a cognitive shift (Costa & Garmston, 2002; Schon, 1987). We are not certain how it happens, but that it happens is evident in people's physical and emotional reactions. Facial expressions and posture changes are observable, and an energy to do things differently and right is evident.

Reflections on Entitlement: A Pine Hills Elementary School Conversation

Recognition of one's feelings or reactions is a first step to being able to constructively deal with issues of oppression in our schools and communities. Let us return to the discussion between our two educator colleagues from Maple View School District's Pine Hills Elementary School, and we see that Joan is identifying how she has acknowledged her feelings and has begun to examine the deeper issues of how students are performing. Joan is becoming receptive to how she can make constructive choices to influence the learning of students:

Connie: It sure seems to me that you have personalized this entire presentation. I sat at the same table as you, but had a very different reaction.

Joan: What do you mean?

Connie: I related her presentation to our current work on serving the needs of underperforming students. Yes, I do feel a twinge when we discuss systems of oppression, but I have begun to focus on her comment, "When you feel that twinge of emotion, look to see if you are on the verge of deeper learning." For me, the deeper learning is involved with how can we become effective with students who are not being successful in our schools.

Joan: Well, if their parents don't even care . . .

Connie: Wait just a minute! You are feeding into just what the presenter described.

Joan: What do you mean?

Connie: By focusing solely on the parents, you are not considering the power and authority we have as educators. If we believe our students have the capacity to learn, then we can learn ways in which to teach them. You do remember the EdTrust PowerPoint presentation, don't you? The one in which numerous schools with demographics just like ours are being very successful? It is about our taking responsibility to research, to find, and to use materials and approaches that work for our students and us.

Joan is being coached by Connie to look beyond her initial, personal reaction and examine her underlying assumptions about her students and their parents. Joan is on the verge of being able to exercise direct influence over how she views and works with her students and their parents. At this point, Joan, if she so chooses, will be more able and willing to begin examining her practice—the one thing over which she has total control—to see how she can work differently with her students. As Joan experiences this transition, she will feel more empowered. Her empowerment is her personal transformation.

■ Reflective Activity

What is your reaction to this section on anger, guilt, or confidence?

_____

_____

_____

_____

_____

If you were to design a desired shift in thinking for yourself, what would it look like?

_____

_____

_____

_____

_____

_____

Reflections on Entitlement: Oppression, Entitlement, or Self-Determination and Personal Responsibility?

The types of comments Joan made in the previous vignette are not new or surprising. They proliferate in the conversations that we hear in informal settings in schools at all levels (i.e., prekindergarten to university). People who make such comments do not seem to understand that people's experiences in our society vary greatly. For example, we have made presentations in which the demographics of schools and the inequities that exist are presented in quantitative detail. However, the same question arises almost every time. No amount of data can forestall it. The most compelling information on the underachievement of children from low socioeconomic backgrounds cannot derail it. The question is as follows:

> This is all well and good; however, how am I supposed to react when a student approaches me to contribute to a fund for Latino/Latina scholarships? Now, I am a fair person. I came from a poor background. Why can't we just contribute to scholarships for all students of need?

Other times, it is in the following form: "As a school board member or administrator, it gets real tiring having these special-interest groups assail us at board meetings! Please, what are we to do with these groups? Why can't we treat everyone the same?" The following is another example:

> Why do we educators have to take the blame for students not achieving? Why doesn't anyone look at which students are the behavior problems in this school? Has it occurred to anyone that these are the kids who are low achievers? You don't think this is an accident, do you?

We do not doubt that the questions are often sincere and earnest. We do not doubt that these educators, who represent both genders, many ages, and many cultural backgrounds, sincerely have these questions. However, one thing is inescapable: There is always an underlying tension that appears to be anger, guilt, or frustration. Our response often begins with the following statement: "An important aspect of diversity training is not so much what we learn about other people, but what we learn about our reactions to other people."

It is our observation that those who are privileged or entitled are often unwilling or unable to see the oppression that others experience (Bohn & Sleeter, 2000). Therefore, like Joan, when they are confronted with new data or perspectives, their reactions are expressed as anger, guilt, or frustration. The inability to see how others experience our schools is very limiting. Several cultures acknowledge this limitation with maxims such as "You cannot understand me until you have walked a mile in my shoes." Not being able to see our entitlement limits our ability to move forward in our own learning to educate children from backgrounds different from ours to high levels of achievement. The damaging effects of racism and other forms of oppression are exceeded only by the unwillingness or inability of dominant society to make the commitment use one's entitlement to end oppression.

Self-Determination and Personal Responsibility: From Feelings to Action

The feelings of anger, guilt, and self-confidence represented in Figures 5.1 and 5.2 have behavioral counterparts—namely oppression, entitlement, and self-determination/personal responsibility. Figure 5.3 represents a range of reactions, from oppression to entitlement, with self-determination and personal responsibility being the midpoint. In the same way that anger and guilt are opposite feelings and reactions, oppression and entitlement are opposite behaviors, and they too can lead to one being paralyzed and dysfunctional in making effective changes for our schools. The middle point of this continuum represents self-determination for those who are from historically oppressed groups, and it represents personal responsibility for those who are from privileged and entitled groups. The common denominator for both the oppressed and the entitled members is that they have constructive, functional choices to make and actions to take as educators.

Figure 5.3 Oppression-Entitlement Continuum

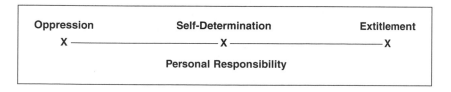

Oppression is the consequence of racism, sexism, ethnocentrism, or heterosexism. Overt acts of oppression serve to deny the benefits of society to people based on their membership in a group. Throughout our country's history, visible acts of oppression in schools include tracking programs that result in low or no mobility for specific ethnic or racial groups, chronic achievement gaps among groups, suspension and expulsion rates that are disparate among groups, and curricula that represent only dominant society. Less obvious, although no less pernicious, acts of oppression include lowered expectations, biased testing, and ethnocentric history and literature textbooks. Biased testing creates a reverse affirmative action. Ethnocentric textbooks have given the dominant society a mythical view of its role in the growth of this country and made all others invisible, exotic, or dehumanized. These practices are a significant part of our history and culture that, for too long, dominant society has tried to ignore. The very act of ignoring these issues is a choice reserved for only the entitled and privileged.

It is our experience that when issues of oppression are raised, many of us who are from historically oppressed groups sometimes become agitated and angry that others in the group are either naive or resistant to hearing about our legacy of oppression. For people from historically oppressed groups, the struggle is to recognize systemic and systematic oppression and to commit oneself to self-determination. Possibly the ultimate oppression is for one to accept the notion that the system is so hopelessly racist, sexist, ethnocentric, or heterosexist that there is nothing one can do. This position robs one of personal power. Conversely, people from these historically oppressed groups who understand oppression are able to confront dysfunctional systems and network with others to take control of their personal and professional lives. They are not seduced by tokenism, but work with their colleagues to become leaders in developing policies and practices that serve the historically underserved.

The challenge for many of us who confront the concept of entitlement for the first time is that the benefits are often unrecognized and unacknowledged. The privileges of entitlement—to the entitled—are often invisible and appear to be just the way the world is. Entitled people may see oppression, be disgusted by it, and never consider that they have directly benefited from the systematic oppression of others. To become aware of and to acknowledge entitlement is a sign of growth and strength. To understand both oppression and entitlement is the first step to self-determination and personal responsibility.

Figure 5.4 presents oppression and entitlement as being similar in that they are dysfunctional. The functional alternatives are self-determination and personal responsibility.

Figure 5.4   Functional and Dysfunctional Reactions to Oppression and Entitlement

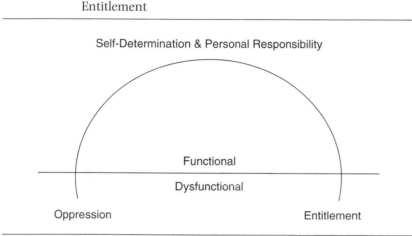

Self-Determination & Personal Responsibility

Functional

Dysfunctional

Oppression   Entitlement

For entitled people, after they understand and recognize oppression and the benefits of entitlement, they then have a moral choice to make. To do nothing, once informed, is tantamount to the immoral position of conspirator. The moral position is to commit oneself to end oppression. Although entitled people may work with oppressed groups to oppose acts of oppression, their major responsibility is to work within schools and districts to raise the consciousness of the uninformed entitled. They focus their energies on changing policies, practices, and behaviors that perpetuate oppression and entitlement, recognizing that the two are inextricably interconnected.

Similar to the discussion about movement from anger and guilt to confidence, educators who transcend the oppression and entitlement responses and, instead, opt for self-determination and personal responsibility have demonstrated the willingness to reflect on their practices for the purpose of providing their students access to high-quality educational experiences. Educators such as these demonstrate the ability to reflect on their practices while working with students, as well as to think back on their practices, for the purpose of continuous improvement. These educators have made the shift in thinking from cultural destructiveness, cultural incapacity, and cultural blindness to cultural precompetence and cultural competence. The language of these educators shifts from "why these students cannot succeed" to statements such as "These are different ways in which I would like to approach my work with our students."

Informed, entitled people understand that to confront unacknowledged privileges inherent in institutional values, policies, and practices that perpetuate disparity takes keen insight and commitment to moral authority. School leaders can be pivotal in ensuring that we, all of us, are part of the discussions about diversity. Let us revisit Joan and Connie, who have been talking about these issues, and see how they are handling these topics:

Joan: Okay, so I am beginning to understand. My feelings are more about resistance than anything. I can see that now. I can't say that I am totally comfortable with this whole notion yet, but I can appreciate that we have to do something. I am beginning to understand your feedback that I want to "short-circuit" the system of learning about cultural proficiency.

Connie: With that, we can make a start. How is it you recognize, within yourself, that you have been avoiding the deeper learning?

Joan: Well, it has to do with the presentation the other day. I have been thinking—no, hoping—that all of this fuss about diversity was that I was going to need to learn particular strategies in working with low-performing students.

Connie: How do you see it now?

Joan: I am not totally certain, but I know it has to involve my looking at what I expect from my students, how I interact with them, and my knowledge of how students learn. In some ways, it is as if I am starting all over again as a teacher.

Connie: Yes, it is about learning and unlearning; however, the main difference between now and when we began our roles as educators is that we have a storehouse of knowledge of what does and what does not work.

Joan: Well, this diversity training must be awfully burdensome for you.

Connie: How do you mean?

Joan: You already know all of this stuff, don't you?

Connie: Hardly! Though I am a person of color, there is much for me to learn about working with all groups. However, probably the most important role I see for myself is to make sure that I keep these issues on the table for all of us to face. That is a challenge that I welcome.

Joan: Yeah. And, that is a challenge I have to share with you. It is like the speaker said the other day: "We have to approach each of these students like we would want people to approach our own children." That sure makes it personal.

Being culturally precompetent is often described as knowing what you do not know. It is not having the answers but being able to know when current practices are not serving students. Cultural precompetent educators demonstrate a willingness to learn about their students' cultures, learning styles, and communities in which they live. Culturally competent educators reflect on their practices using the lens of the five essential elements—assessing their cultural knowledge, valuing diversity, managing the dynamics of difference, adapting to diversity, and institutionalizing cultural knowledge. Culturally competent educators are committed to the inside-out approach of cultural proficiency as they continuously examine their values and behaviors and seek to improve their practices.

■ Reflective Activity

In Chapter 3, we invited you to identify three bold steps for cultural proficiency at your school. How has this chapter informed that process for you?

_____

_____

_____

_____

_____

_____

What questions do you have to guide your continued learning?

_____

_____

_____

_____

_____

_____

Dr. Campbell left that day confident the Maple View Elementary School had begun the task of moving forward with learning how to move the staff and the school toward being culturally proficient. She sat in her car for a few minutes to reflect on today's session. She thought to herself,

> I think the leaders at this school are beginning to view reform as a very personal choice of transformation. I do know that learning about entitlement and privilege will be a continuous challenge for all of us. However, we have to continuously ask ourselves, "How is it that I can change my practices to benefit our students."

Chapters 2 through 5 have provided you with the tools of culturally competent practice and the opportunity to reflect on your own practice. Part III, Chapters 6 and 7, provides you with techniques and tools to use in professional development. Chapter 6 provides an overview of the forms of conversation we use in our schools and an activity to use in professional development sessions with your colleagues. Chapter 7 describes a lab protocol you and your colleagues can use to ingrain the tools of cultural proficiency into everyday practice.

Part III

Professional Development for Organizational Change

6

The Art and Science of Conversation

A Crucial Skill for the Culturally Competent Leader

Listening . . . requires not only open eyes and ears, but open hearts and minds. We do not really see through our eyes or hear through our ears, but through our beliefs. . . . It is not easy, but it is the only way to learn what it might feel like to be someone else and the only way to start the dialogue.

—Lisa Delpit (1995, p. 46)

Skillful Use of Communication Channels

Dr. Barbara Campbell and colleagues set forth a vision for the Maple View School District to commit its effort and resources to provide a high-quality education for all students that enables each one to achieve or exceed high academic and performance standards. Dr. Campbell committed to leading the district to examine behaviors and policies through the lens of cultural proficiency. In Chapters 2 through 5, we had the opportunity to witness many conversations of Maple View educators and community members as they have learned the basic tools of cultural proficiency—the guiding principles, the continuum, the five essential elements, and the barriers of anger and guilt.

In the vignettes of the preceding chapters, we have seen that culturally proficient leaders are intentional in the use of their school's formal and informal communication networks. These leaders, who are administrators and teachers, are aware of the power of person-to-person communication. They understand that building effective relationships involves guiding their colleagues to understand the "why's" of individual and group behaviors. Culturally proficient leaders structure faculty meetings, department and grade level meetings, and meetings with parents and community members in such a way as to maximize person-to-person communication. These same leaders realize that when they foster effective communication in their ongoing work, they are increasing the likelihood that the requisite skills and attitudes will carry over into the informal conversations among their colleagues. Culturally proficient school leaders see that relationship building through conversation is an important component in developing schools responsive to the needs of diverse and ever-changing communities.

In her powerful book, *Turning to One Another: Simple Conversations to Restore Hope to the Future*, Margaret Wheatley (2002) tells us that conversation is an ancient art form that comes naturally to us as humans, but that human beings are becoming increasingly isolated and fragmented and need one another more than ever. Schools are often isolating places in which dozens of adults spend 8 to 10 hours per day in relatively autonomous activities and interactions with their students but rarely spend time in effective conversations with other adults. Teachers are in their classrooms with 20 to 35 students, whereas administrators and counselors are consumed with their daily tasks. Formal meetings and professional development sessions are frequently for one-way communication of information. Too often, we are in regimented situations that provide little time or opportunity to nurture deep, substantive conversations about our practices as educators.

Communication within schools occurs in both formal and informal settings. Formal settings include the aforementioned faculty meetings, parent-teacher meetings, grade level and department meetings, and formal classroom instruction. Wenger (1998) described our more informal communication networks in terms of communities of practice. Often, our communities of practice are composed of the networks of communication that occur in the hallways, the parking lots, the faculty lounge, or any other informal setting.

Conversation is one of the most important forms of social behavior in our schools, but it receives little attention in either its formal or informal settings. Some conversation processes promote communication, whereas others seemingly end in miscommunication or noncommunication. Cultural proficiency requires understanding and mastery of the modes of conversation that promote effective communication. In this chapter, we discuss conversation and its relationship to communication, understanding, and cultural proficiency. We present four modes of conversation described by Senge (1994) and consider how they relate to one another and how use of different modes of conversation either promotes or obstructs cultural proficiency in school settings. The chapter concludes with exercises for dialogic practice designed to assist educational leaders who choose to move their schools and districts toward culturally proficient practices.

Organizations Are Relationships

Our exploration of conversation as a means to becoming culturally proficient begins with an exploration of the concept of organizations. Traditionally, we study organizations at two levels, structural and systemic (Cross, 1989, Heifetz, 1994; Owens, 1995; Sergiovanni, 1992; Wheatley, 1992, 2002). Weick (1979) provides us with a framework for understanding the systemic nature of organizations:

> Most "things" in organizations are actually relationships, variables tied together in a systematic fashion. Events, therefore, depend on the strength of these ties, the direction of influence, the time it takes for information in the form of differences to move around circuits. (p. 88)

Viewing schools as relationships linked together as circuits is useful in understanding the interconnectedness of human social organizations and how information flows through them. Rather than schools being regarded only as building sites, Weick (1979) offers a view of organizations—in our case, schools—that are grounded in the values and beliefs of individuals. He states,

> The word organization is a noun, and it is also a myth. If you look for an organization you won't find it. What you will find is that there are events, linked together, that transpire within concrete walls and these sequences, their pathways, and their timing are the forms we erroneously make into substances when we talk about an organization. Just as the skin is a misleading boundary for marking off where a person ends and the environment starts, so are the walls of an organization. Events inside organizations and organisms are locked into causal circuits that extend beyond these artificial boundaries. (p. 88)

Consistent with Weick (1979), Maturana and Varela (1992) extend our understanding beyond the mechanics of linkages and circuits in relationships toward an inward journey of life. They describe the organization of biological life as "autopoetic" or self-organizing. The organization is a product of its own patterns, procedures, and processes and its responses or reactions to its environment and to external interactions. In other words, there is no separation between what it is and what it does. They note,

> That living beings have an organization, of course, is proper not only to them but also to everything we can analyze as a system. What is distinctive about them, however, is that their organization is such that their only product is themselves, with no separation between producer and product. The being and doing of an autopoetic unity are inseparable and this is their specific mode of organization. (p. 48)

Organizations exist within the hearts and minds of the people who are part of them; they are the collective values and beliefs of those people. Organizational values and beliefs, in turn, are manifested in people's actions. The four forms of conversation provide varying opportunities to coalesce people's values and beliefs, to shape collective understanding, to reveal people's underlying values and beliefs, and to open them to change.

The Essence of Communication:
Exchange of Information and Meaning

When people engage in effective communication with one another, they authentically share information and construct meaning together. This social construction of meaning is the essence of communication, and to understand it, we return to the example of the conversation that began Chapter 5. Maple View Elementary teachers Joan Stephens and Connie Barkley are talking about the cultural proficiency seminar in which they recently participated. Joan is struggling to understand her deep emotional reactions to the session and asks Connie, a colleague she knows she can trust, to hear her out and help her make sense of her feelings.

In this conversation, Connie is guiding Joan to internally process her own beliefs and assumptions about racism, the achievement gap, and her own sense of responsibility. This form of communication is at the heart of effective conversation and is fundamental for leadership in culturally proficient schools. Traditionally, we think of communication as the transmission and reception of information by means of speech, writing, or other representations of language. Maturana and Varela (1992) portray communication as an internal process that is socially constructed. In the conversation between Connie and Joan, Joan is at the point of discovering several things. First, she may be learning to recognize what she does not know—in this case, school-based instances of racism. Second, she has become aware that discussions about issues related to diversity engender within her deep feelings that she has ignored. Third, and most important, she has the opportunity to learn about the experiences of others in her school community. As Joan becomes receptive to the experiences and perspectives of others, she will be better equipped to engage in the effective exchange of information with others.

Most of us are like Joan in that we experience this inner communications process when encountering an object or a situation that is alien or unfamiliar. In Joan's case, it is the seminar on cultural proficiency that is triggering her internal sense-making process. For many people, this occurs when they experience something that is unfamiliar or foreign to them. In their struggles to understand the experience, they process the information internally within the frame they have available—the context of their own life experiences. In such a situation, what is said may not be what is heard. Communication depends not only on what is transmitted but also on the internal sense-making process of the person who receives it. To Joan's credit, she is courageously reaching out to Connie and wants her help in checking her own understanding of what was presented the previous evening and her own reaction to the presentation. As we return to the conversation, Joan and Connie are engaging in what Senge (1994) refers to as "skilled discussion."

■ Modes of Conversing

To better help us to understand the connection between communication/conversation and cultural proficiency, we introduce what Senge (1994) identified as raw debate, polite discussion, skilled discussion, and dialogue as the four forms of conversation most likely to occur in organizations (see Figure 6.1). Each form of conversation has distinct purposes and produces specific results, and knowledge of these distinctions can be important for leaders intent on leading their schools or districts toward cultural proficiency. As you read this section, reflect on the narratives from the previous chapters that struck you in particular ways. You will be able to place those narratives at various points along Senge's conversation continuum. To illustrate the four forms of conversation, we continue Joan and Connie's conversation in four alternative scenarios: raw debate, polite discussion, skilled discussion, and dialogue.

Figure 6.1   Senge's Conversation Continuum

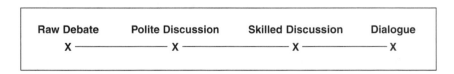

Raw debate represents complete advocacy and, although often polarizing, can identify people's stand on issues. A form of conversation that is rarely helpful in the exploration of issues and ideas is *polite discussion*. Polite discussion, prevalent in schools, is characterized by masking of one's feelings or reactions to issues under consideration. *Skilled discussion* involves a balance of advocacy and inquiry and is most efficient and effective in school settings. *Dialogue*, the opposite of raw debate, involves an intentional discussion in which participants, over time, seek to gain a shared understanding of a topic or issue.

If you review the tables in Chapter 4 or the conversations in Chapter 5, you will see examples of these four forms of conversation. As you reread the tables in Chapter 4 from left to right, you will distinguish movement from raw debate to skilled discussion and to the potential for dialogue.

The four conversation forms, depending on the topic, the purpose, and the situation, are useful in reaching understandings and taking action. To use them effectively, it is helpful to understand both their purpose and their potential outcomes.

Raw Debate

This form of communication is represented by complete advocacy on the part of each member engaged in the conversation. Each member holds to a predetermined position. Participants listen as a matter of strategy. Raw debate results in winners and losers. This form of conversation can be active or benign. An active form is evident when participants knowingly stake their positions on the issues and relentlessly advocate for their viewpoints. The benign form of debate is evident in hierarchical organizations in which agendas and executive actions forecast predetermined positions and are used to overwhelm opposing ideas.

If Joan and Connie extend their conversation into active raw debate, it might take the following course:

Joan: I have a lot of trouble with that "What are you willing to do" position! I am willing to become a teacher. I am willing to keep my credential current through professional reading and university coursework. I am willing to come to class prepared. My question is, "Why don't their parents care enough to make sure their kids come to school to learn?"

Connie: I think that is a fair question. My question to us, not just to you, is "What is our role in working with the parents?"

Joan: I didn't become an educator to become a social worker! My responsibilities are very clear—to teach!

Connie: Well, it seems to me that you have a very narrow view of our work and that you are unwilling to entertain any reasonable suggestion.

If it continues, this conversation will most likely devolve into a contentious point-counterpoint conversation until a winner is declared or one party relents. Let's see if polite discussion has any promise for Joan and Connie.

Polite Discussion

This form of conversation is similar to debate in that participants seemingly agree with one another but in reality do not. Speakers mask their positions in an attempt to show politeness, never truly revealing their thinking. Polite discussions occur in at least two contexts. In a face-to-face conversation, polite discussions are often filled with words such as "but," "except," "only," and "however." Participants are careful not to reveal their true values and feelings but rather to participate in a dance of deception. Polite discussion often occurs when people participate in a discussion, not revealing their feelings or opinions, but when encountering their colleagues in the hallways or in parking lots, they have no difficulty expressing their true reactions. Had Joan and Connie chosen to continue their conversation as a polite discussion, we may have heard something like the following:

Joan: Well, that cultural proficiency presentation yesterday certainly was interesting, but . . .

Connie: What do you mean "interesting, but . . ."?

Joan: Oh, it was okay. It's just that when you have been here as long as I have, you learn that every few years some consultant comes in and reminds us of what we need to do to be successful with these kids in our classes. I just check it off my list of "diversity experiences."

Connie: It sounds like it was a waste of your time.

Joan: Oh no, I just know the game.

Connie: The game? I'm not getting your point.

Joan: Oh, it's nothing in particular. By the way, Connie, tell Dr. Campbell that I'll be glad to serve on any committee she organizes. Tell her she can always count on me!

What do you think? At this point in the conversation, do you think it is likely that Joan is willing to do the deep internal work of integrating the five essential elements of cultural competence as standards for her work as an educator? It appears that she is closing herself to that opportunity and politely choosing superficial compliance as her path.

By moving their conversation to the level of skilled discussion, Connie and Joan have a heightened opportunity to use conversation to explore each other's support and resistance to issues related to diversity.

Skilled Discussion

Skilled discussion includes a balance of inquiry and advocacy and is a productive way of conversing. Leaders who are effective in skilled discussion balance their conversations by seeking to understand others' perspectives. They openly reveal their own positions on topics and seek to understand others' viewpoints through active questioning. They are aware of their own assumptions and beliefs and know how they express them in meetings. They encourage everyone's participation in meetings. They seek to gain multiple perspectives on issues. These leaders guide discussants to critically examine their own beliefs and assumptions. Joan and Connie might have the following skilled discussion:

Joan: Connie, your comment that "we are not observers, we are participants in the change process" is disconcerting, at best.

Connie: I'm not sure what you mean, Joan.

Joan: I've been on the curriculum committee for the past 3 years. I've been the one to press our colleagues to actively integrate the teaching standards into our daily work. I don't see myself as an observer.

Connie: On those issues, you are definitely a facilitator and supporter. My comments are about your reaction to the topic of racism. My interest isn't to put you into a corner, but to be responsive to your request for me to listen to your reaction to the cultural proficiency presentation. How can I be most helpful to you?

Joan: Good point! You're doing it by keeping me focused. As difficult as this is, I do appreciate it!

Although this part of the narrative does not indicate shared understanding, it demonstrates the ability to stay engaged in the conversation. Both Joan and Connie experience the opportunity to gain an understanding of each other's position on the topic at hand, and they both seek an understanding of each other's feelings and reactions as they emerge in the conversation. Dialogue may provide Connie and Joan the opportunity to take a next step in the process of substantive, deep, enlightening, and effective conversation.

Dialogue

Dialogue is oriented toward inquiry for the purpose of developing a collective understanding of a given topic. Dialogue attempts to bridge the perceived or real differences between speakers. In this mode of conversation, participants seek to understand others' viewpoints and experiences and the underlying reasons for others' thoughts and actions, and they reflect on their own viewpoints and experiences. Thus, participants in dialogue gain information and insight not only about others but also about themselves. Connie and Joan might have the following dialogue:

Joan: You know, this topic of racism perplexes the daylight out of me.

Connie: Perplexes?

Joan: As you've noted, I'm resistant to the information, and at the same time I'm aware of intense reactions roiling within me. This may blow you away, but I'd like to learn more about racism.

Connie: No, I'm not astounded, but I am pleased. Yes, *racism* evokes strong emotional reactions, but it's also a term that has specific meaning.

Joan: Can you give me any tips on how I can get started?

Connie: You've done the first step, Joan. You've taken responsibility for your own learning. And, yes, I do have several readings I can recommend. More important, would you be interested in working with me to organize a group of people who'll be willing to commit to reading about and discussing racism?

In our work, we teach two basic dialogic skills that could contribute to Connie and Joan's dialogic group's conversation. At the basic level of dialogue, participants discuss with one another the "why" of their beliefs or actions. As Connie and Joan's dialogic group forms, they will share viewpoints about their reading. They most likely will first summarize the author's intent, and then they will react to the material. An important component of their sharing of reactions will be for them to probe within themselves and with others as to why they experience those reactions. To move to a deeper level of understanding, they will ask and respond to questions that begin with the "where," "when," and "who" of the sources of their beliefs and assumptions. Connie and Joan and other participants will emerge with an understanding of their various readings, a deeper understanding of racism, and, most important, a recognition of how their individual belief systems are developing.

Examining one's own beliefs and assumptions is an essential skill in becoming culturally proficient. After all, cultural proficiency involves an inward journey in which one increasingly understands his or her own beliefs and actions and the impact that those beliefs and actions have on others. A commitment to the process of dialogue is one way for people to deepen their knowledge of themselves and others. Often, discussions on issues such as racism, privilege, and entitlement are held in a debate format in which positions become increasingly polarized. The consequence of raw debate is the creation of winners and losers and not the development of understanding. As Freire (1999) states, "Only dialogue truly communicates" (p. 45).

Education is a profession grounded in communication. We communicate with our students, the parents of our students, and one another. Conversation is composed of a set of skills that, when practiced, can be improved. The following exercise is a successful process we recommend for your use in leading groups to understand the appropriate use of the four conversation modes. It is not a time-consuming activity. It can be used as a professional development activity or in grade level, department, or school faculty meetings. Once you have conducted the activity with colleagues, it is easy to practice any one or a combination of skills in future meetings. Culturally proficient leaders, as we have indicated throughout this book, are intentional in their work with colleagues, which is why we commend this activity to your use.

Practicing Conversation Skills

First, have participants review and discuss the conversation continuum. Then, place them in dyads (pairs) for the purpose of beginning a dialogue. The facilitator suggests the topic for this activity. It is important that the topic be general enough to allow for dialogue to ensue. It is our experience that the topic of change usually works well as an initial topic of discussion. Change is one of those topics that affects everyone—personally and professionally. It is important that the topic not be one rooted in debate. For example, selecting the emotive topic of racism is not advised for groups beginning this process of discovery. Difficult topics such as racism can be dealt with as participants master the various modes of conversation.

Instruct participants to move away from tables, facing their partners. The activity is conducted in three rounds. Each round builds on the preceding rounds to provide scaffolding for participant learning.

Round 1, limited to 3 minutes, is an open discussion in which participants are given no guidelines or rules for their conversation. Participants are to engage in conversation as they might in any usual professional setting. As mentioned previously, we suggest the topic of conversation be about change.

This round serves two purposes. First, participants warm to the activity. Second, it provides the facilitator with immediate data about how the participants engage in conversation. As they converse, the facilitator listens to the participants' word selection, their tone of voice, and the rhythm of their interaction. All three factors play major roles in a successful conversation. Questions, particularly those beginning with the word "why," are important indicators of the beginnings of a successful dialogic conversation. A courteous exchange of comments can indicate that the participants are engaged in polite discussion. A fast rhythm with few or no questions asked may indicate a debate is in progress.

At the end of the 3 minutes, instruct the group to stop all interaction, and provide a general critique of the conversational patterns you have observed. Often in the first round, participants fail to listen to one another: They cut into each other's sentences, advocate for points of view, and fail to negotiate differences. Pursuit of collective understanding seldom occurs in this round. Most groups in this round begin conversation with the rhythm of a debate, which is extremely fast. Encourage them to slow the pace and listen to each other's words.

Round 2 is a controlled conversation session for which the facilitator sets certain rules. Each participant is given 90 seconds to continue discussing the topic of change while the partner sits and only listens. Overt physical gestures or sounds of agreement or disagreement are not permitted during this round. The facilitator keeps track of time and signals the appropriate moment when participants switch roles. At the end of the round, the facilitator halts all conversation and initiates a debriefing of the process. We have found the following question to be effective in beginning the debriefing session: "What are your insights as a result of this exercise?"

Most newcomers to dialogic conversation find this step to be extremely difficult because of old habits of jumping into the conversation without listening to what others have to say. Often, participants are startled by what they learn from this round. First, they have difficulty believing how slowly time seems to pass during the allotted 90 seconds. Second, they become aware of an inner voice that wants to rush into the conversation before the other person has finished commenting. For many, it is the first time to be aware of how little they listen to one another because of their unwillingness to silence their inner voices and focus on what others have to offer. For the first time, they are aware of their continuous orientation to advocate a point and hold ground rather than becoming involved in inquiry of one another's perspectives on an issue.

Round 3 begins participants in a structured process to learn skills of dialogue. Allow 20 to 25 minutes for this round. Participants are encouraged to ask clusters of three to five "why" questions to uncover the speaker's assumptions and predispositions about the topic. For example, when participants discover that they associate control with the topic of change, they may ask, "Why is it necessary to be in control of change?" They may also ask, "Why is control important?" and "Why do we need to control the lives of others?"

The second step is for participants to ask "where" and "when" questions of one another. These questions help participants see themselves at a place in time. Understanding of one's own assumptions and beliefs can be revealed as one reflectively responds to questions such as "Where did I learn that change was good or bad?" "When in my life did I develop such attitudes?" and "Where (or when) did you get the notion that change is controllable?"

The third step involves asking the question of "who?" This is extremely powerful. A simple question such as "From whom did you learn this?" gives one insight into beliefs and values derived from relationships earlier in one's own life. Identifying these relationships affords participants the opportunity to understand when, where, and from whom their values and beliefs were learned. It has been our experience that participants, upon discovering these where, when, and who connections, discover that many of their values and behaviors function like unspoken contracts with people important in their earlier lives. This knowledge alone provides people with the opportunity to retain and modify values and beliefs.

Debrief the three rounds by asking participants the following questions:

1. What are the contrasting characteristics of the three rounds of conversation in which you were engaged?

2. What seemed comfortable in each round? What was challenging in each round?

3. How do you compare the third round, dialogue, with the conversations that take place in your school setting?

Bohm (1996), a leading proponent of the benefits of dialogue, indicates that for true dialogue to occur, we must be willing to invest sufficient time. We know that in our schools, time is precious. Although we do not have unlimited time and other resources for professional development, there are several steps leaders must take. We have found that in a short period of time, participants can learn to navigate the continuum of conversation well enough to have the beginnings of good dialogue on difficult issues, such as racism, entitlement, and oppression. By understanding how to steer colleagues through the four modes of conversation, leaders are able to use dialogue as a way of gaining understanding of their own and others' attitudes and values about issues of race, ethnicity, class, gender, sexual orientation, language proficiency, and ability.

Educators who understand the bases for their own values can choose to change their behaviors. Similarly, these educators can also examine organizational policies and practices for underlying biases. In Chapter 7, we discuss the laboratory protocol technique for educators to examine their policies and practices.

7

Leading in a Culture of Learning and Transformative Change

[I]mprovement is more of a function of learning to do the right thing in the setting where you work than it is of what you know when you start to do the work. . . . Organizations that improve do so because they create and nurture agreement on what is worth achieving, and they set in motion the internal processes by which people progressively learn how to do what they need to do in order to achieve what is worthwhile. Importantly, such organizations select, reward, and retain people based on their willingness to engage the purposes of the organization and to acquire the learning that is required to achieve those purposes. Improvement occurs through organized social learning.

Experimentation and discovery can be harnessed to social learning by connecting people with new ideas to each other in an environment in which ideas are subject to scrutiny, measured against the collective purposes of the organization, and tested by the history of what has already been learned and known.

—Richard Elmore (2000, p. 25)

Learning How to Be a Culturally Proficient Leader

Dr. Barbara Campbell had been in meetings throughout the day. Early that morning, she met over breakfast with Gary Thompson, Maple View's mayor, and several members of the chamber of commerce. They were making final plans for the "grand opening" of the new Boys and Girls Club on Main Street in the east-side area. The city purchased the old Central Market building, which had been empty for 8 years. Barbara had worked hard for the past 2 years to bring this dream to reality. The club would be a place where students living on the east side of the city could have access to many of the educational supports and opportunities that students on the west side took for granted. The club would be a safe afterschool center that would offer tutoring, counseling, a library, a computer workshop for desktop publishing and filmmaking, and a sports gym. Barbara had started her day with a great sense of accomplishment, and she was looking forward to the ceremony this weekend.

Following her breakfast meeting, Barbara returned to the district office and met with several staff members to work on preparing the district's budget for review by the board of education. At this point in the school year, preparing the district's budget was requiring a lot of her attention. However, now, with those meetings behind her, she had a little quiet time in her office to prepare for her next meeting. In fewer than 30 minutes, she would be meeting with all eight of the district's principals in what they collectively had begun calling the "leadership lab team." She smiled, thinking back to approximately 8 months ago when the group had decided to meet together each Thursday after school as a district leadership team. That had been a pretty remarkable decision, and it had evolved out of the cultural proficiency seminars they had experienced at the beginning of the school year.

The principals had found that the work of facing up to difficult sociocultural problems in their communities and taking them on was not easy, but they had made a commitment to tackle the work as a group. Barbara had gently but firmly challenged the principals to help their teachers become culturally competent educators as a means of eliminating the achievement gap that they had uncovered as a result of analyzing disaggregated student performance data. That had been another remarkable benchmark. The principals had intuitively sensed the disparities in achievement among different subgroups of students; nonetheless, they were startled by the stark revelations in their data. Barbara recalled the unifying and inspiring impact this discovery had had on the principals. They did not want those results to be their legacy.

By 3:30 p.m., all eight of the principals had arrived at the district office for their weekly gathering. Barbara had arranged to have coffee, cold drinks, and fruit ready for the meeting, and as the principals came into the meeting room, they helped themselves to the refreshments. Barbara was pleased that everyone arrived on time, as usual. Their behavior demonstrated mutual respect and showed that the meeting was important to them. At 4:00 p.m., they were all sitting in a circle ready to begin their leadership lab protocol.

Each week, one of the principals presented an "action-learning case," a description of a cultural proficiency predicament or dilemma with which he or she was struggling. The case presenter also described the type of feedback he or she wanted the group to offer. One of the basic ground rules of the process disallows giving advice or solutions as feedback. Another rule requires all feedback to be framed as a question rather than a statement. The design of the process intentionally provokes the case presenter to be reflective and analytical rather than solution seeking. Advice giving tends to stop reflective analysis and imposes an external solution. The process generally lasts for 1 hour, with approximately 30 minutes of discussion following.

In their early meetings, the group collaborated to define the structure and framework that would guide their lab process. Their joint goal was ambitious. They committed themselves to becoming culturally proficient leaders as individuals and as a group. They also pledged to create the conditions in which cultural proficiency would become an organizational norm in their schools and throughout the district. They agreed that the five principles of cultural proficiency and the cultural proficiency continuum would serve as the benchmarks by which they would assess their progress.

The five principles are as follows:

- Culture is a predominant force in people's lives.
- The dominant culture serves people in varying degrees.
- People have both personal identities and group identities.
- Diversity within cultures is vast and significant.
- Each individual and each group has unique cultural values and needs.

The following are the six points of the cultural proficiency continuum of cultural responses:

- Destructiveness
- Incapacity
- Blindness
- Precompetence
- Competence
- Proficiency

Today's case presenter is Ed Johnson, the principal of Maple View Elementary School. Ed is an African American in his second year as principal. His school is one of the state's "targeted" schools, meaning that students are not achieving "adequate yearly progress" and are "underperforming." Through his analysis of Maple View's student performance data, Ed has discovered that African American boys are consistently the lowest-performing subgroup in all reading skills subtests. Ed has discussed these performance results with several literacy researchers at regional universities, and he has learned of a new research-based instructional process that is showing dramatic results with African American male students. Ed has reviewed the research with Barbara and several teachers who are interested in learning the new instructional strategies. Ed's dilemma is that three veteran teachers who are not involved in implementing the new approach are quite critical of it and have generated concern and resistance among African American parents in the community. The parents are demanding that their children not be involved in this "experiment."

The lab protocol calls for Ed to present the case description within 15 minutes (see Table 7.1). The following 10-minute period is designated as a clarification question-and-answer phase. During this period, Ed is permitted to answer clarifying questions with added information; however, advice couched as a question is not permitted.

The next 15-minute period is allocated to the listeners for discussion and planning of the feedback they will offer Ed. Ed can listen in to the discussions, but he cannot join them. The lab rules require all feedback to be framed as questions that support reflection and inquiry about culturally proficient leadership behaviors that could be helpful in the case. For the final 15-minute segment of the protocol, members of the group offer Ed feedback as questions. The protocol rules call for Ed to listen but not respond to the feedback. One member of the group records the questions so that Ed may consider them more deeply after the meeting.

Table 7.1   Learning Lab Protocol

Presentation of case or dilemma	15 minutes
Why I selected this case or dilemma	
The data I analyzed	
My interpretation of the data – what it means	
Culturally proficient actions I have taken	
Possible next steps	
Assessment of my work	
Reflections on my work	
Feedback I desire	
Listeners pose clarifying questions	10 minutes
Listeners meet and prepare feedback	15 minutes
Listeners offer feedback in question form, and presenter does not respond	15 minutes
Presenter may make a closing remark	1 minute

As the questioning continues, Sam Brewer, the principal of Pine Hills High School, asks, "Ed, what assumptions do you have about the students that will participate in this new approach? And, what assumptions do you have about their parents?" Ed nods and turns toward Barbara, who asks, "What information do the parents have about this new approach, Ed? Who have they talked with about it? Why are they calling it experimental?" After a brief pause, Cheryl Robinson, the principal at Greenview Elementary, asks, "How are the teachers who will use this program being trained? What do they know about the research behind the program? Have they talked with the researchers who are promoting this approach?" Then, just as the feedback segment is ending, George Gonzalez, the principal at Main Street Elementary, signals that he has one last question: "Ed, would you put your own kid in this program?" At that moment, everyone looks at Ed as he sits back in his chair. Barbara intervenes and suggests that the group take a brief break and return in 10 minutes for their discussion.

Before anyone else moves, Ed leans forward and quietly says, "Thanks, everybody. You've given me a lot to think about. This has been really helpful and I've got a lot of stuff to process. Thanks." Oscar Medina, the principal at Maple View High School, hands Ed the list of questions he has recorded during the lab process. Ed thanks him and smiles as he tells Oscar,

> Wow, I feel like I've had cold water splashed on my face. There are so many things about this new reading approach that I wasn't noticing, and now, I'm more aware of them. Thanks again for the list, Oscar. This will help me focus my thinking.

Ed's perceptions about his dilemma are beginning to shift. The questions that his colleagues have posed in the lab process will help him reconsider and reflectively analyze the situation through the lens of cultural proficiency. The action-learning lab process that Dr. Campbell and the Maple View principals use every week offers them a continuing opportunity to participate in a professional culture in which they are developing the confidence and skill to collaboratively question, analyze, and critique their own actions and to give and receive feedback that helps them refocus their leadership behaviors into a repertoire of productive and culturally proficient practices.

The theory guiding the use of the action-learning lab is that the knowledge and skill of culturally proficient leadership are complex and not easily codified or disseminated. Culturally proficient leadership is not routine, and questions of improving practice are not simple. The structure of the lab process acknowledges the transformative nature of personal, professional, and organizational change necessary to achieve cultural proficiency. Becoming a culturally proficient leader requires individuals to go beyond improving their behavior and reframing their thinking, to altering their perceptions about who they are and what their purpose is. The action-learning lab supports such a transformation by engaging participants in progressively deeper and more robust reflection on three personally defining questions:

- Why do I want to be different from who I am now?
- How do I have to be different?
- What will be the indicators to me that I am different?

The five essential elements discussed in Chapter 4 are the benchmarks that provide a gauge of culturally proficient leadership practice. The leverage points for change for each essential element in Chapter 4 offer a tool that a leader can use to assess the degree to which his or her own personal values and behaviors exemplify the essential elements of culturally proficient behavior. The rubrics also reveal the progress toward cultural proficiency of a school's or district's policies and practices.

To fully realize the behaviors described implicit in the five essential elements of culturally proficient practice, an individual must first develop an awareness or self-consciousness about his or her actions and their consequences and results. The description of the action-learning lab process in which Barbara Campbell and the Maple View principals participated offers an illustration of an individual who is becoming more aware of his actions and their consequences. Through the reflective questions of his colleagues, Ed Johnson, the young principal presenting his action-learning case, was able to become an observer of his own actions, reflectively analyze those actions, and begin the process of redefining himself and his role. Ed's example presents a view of transformational learning in action. Through transformational learning experiences such as the action-learning lab, practitioners such as Barbara Campbell and the Maple View principals are able to disclose assumptions, values, opinions, emotions, and actions that may be inhibiting productive behavior. By way of social relationships that offer colleagues opportunities to make sense of and transform their actions in the context of their actual practice, continuous examination and reflection on action become habits of practice and organizational norms. As a result, the whole organization becomes smarter, more effective, and progressively better at redefining itself and its purpose.

Transformational Learning

Argyris and Schon (1974, 1996) describe patterns of personal and organizational learning on two levels that they called "single-loop learning" and "double-loop learning." Figure 7.1 displays the relationship between the two patterns. When an individual's or an organization's actions result in undesirable or insufficient results, their efforts to learn how to improve their behavior are single loops, reflecting an analysis of one's actions to improve them or perform them more effectively. The single-loop pattern refers to the one-dimensional examination and change process. In single-loop learning, an individual does not question the appropriateness or "rightness" of an action or the assumptions from which it derives; the single change made is in the manner in which an individual performs the action.

Figure 7.1   Double-Loop Learning (adapted from Argyris, 1990, p. 94)

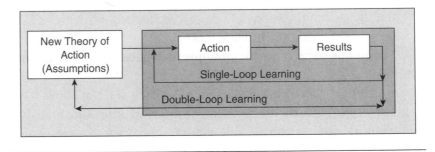

The double-loop pattern reflects a two-dimensional examination and change process. In double-loop learning, an individual questions the assumptions or frames of reference from which the action emerged; the two levels of change are reshaping ways of thinking and learning to do different things. Thus the original dysfunctional behavior or action is abandoned in favor of an entirely different way of thinking about the situation, the action, and the desirable result.

Robert Hargrove (1999) extended the double-loop learning concept to what he calls "triple-loop learning." The triple-loop pattern of learning adds another level of learning by engaging an individual in examining his or her perception of who he or she is and what his or her role or purpose is, and transforming that self-image into a new way of seeing himself or herself and his or her purpose. Hargrove describes the triple-loop pattern as "transformational learning" because, as he argues, it is through such learning experiences that an individual fundamentally transforms his or her way of being and becomes capable of fundamentally different results. Figure 7.2 shows the triple-loop pattern in relation to the single- and double-loop patterns.

Learning to become a culturally proficient leader requires an individual to go beyond improving her behavior and reframing her thinking to shifting her perceptions about who she is and what the

Figure 7.2 Triple-Loop Learning (Transformational Learning, adapted from Hargrove, 1999, p. 2)

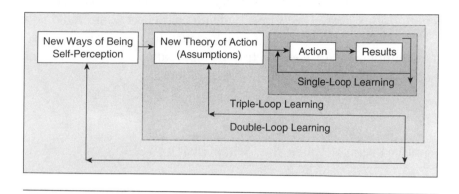

point of her practice is. In the example of Barbara Campbell, Maple View's superintendent, we watch a leader who defines her leadership as culturally proficient practice. In other words, her way of being a leader is to be culturally proficient. She makes it her purpose to help others become culturally proficient, and she consistently supports them in building productive, functional patterns of social interaction. Moreover, Dr. Campbell understands that learning and knowledge transform organizations. Among the principals who participate in the action-learning lab, she has seen individuals make profound changes in how they do their work when they have opportunities to learn within the social context of their daily practice. It is in the learning lab that Dr. Campbell and her administrator colleagues have confronted potentially divisive issues, such as oppression, entitlement, privilege, and anger and guilt. Similarly, they have practiced skills important to effective conversation and explored personal responsibility and self-determination as alternatives to anger and guilt. The labs provide participants the opportunity to explore ways in which to create culturally proficient practices at their schools.

The learning experiences of the lab have reinforced what Dr. Campbell intuitively knew: Face-to-face relationships among people in an organization are the most powerful influencers of individual learning and change, and such relationships are the strongest mechanism for building the organizational knowledge necessary to transform the organization's identity, actions, and results. Indeed, researchers studying organizational learning (Brown & Duguid, 2000; Brown & Isaacs, 2001; Wenger & Snyder, 2000) contend that knowledge of new and better practices bubbles up and flows throughout an organization when there is a supportive infrastructure that assumes organizational learning emerges from the inventive, improvisational, and creative ways in which people interact and form relationships. Coupling this research with the cultural competence continuum (Cross, 1989) offers additional, deeper examinations of practice and provokes leaders to analyze their uses of power, privilege, and entitlement to constructively shape culturally proficient and socially responsible educational organizations.

A Transformative Vision of Maple View School District

Superintendent Barbara Campbell's transformative vision is clear: Maple View School District will exemplify culturally proficient teaching and learning, and every student will achieve academic success.

Recall in Chapter 2 how Barbara's journey to achieve her vision begins with her challenge to the Maple View principals. As she distributes their schools' achievement reports, she points out that the results are disaggregated by student subgroups and states,

> Look at every subgroup and determine who is doing well and who is not succeeding. And then ask yourselves two questions: "Why are we getting these results?" and "Are these the results we want?" It's very important to understand the dynamics in your schools that are producing the results you're getting. Go back and study these results with your teams. Then study your schools. What are your expectations for each subgroup? Are you meeting those expectations? Why?
>
> I want each of you to be prepared to describe the obstacles that seem to be getting in the way of student achievement in each subgroup. I also want you to be ready to discuss how the norms for expected behavior, the structures—like scheduling and grouping, the patterns of activity, and the rules and procedures in the school—may be contributing to the obstacles your students are experiencing. I expect each of you to be prepared to describe the obstacles that seem to be getting in the way of student achievement in each subgroup.
>
> I'm asking you to think about the dynamics of your schools in relation to the five principles of cultural proficiency that support our district mission. And, one other very important thing, I want you to work with your teams to identify five strong values that make your school the school it is.

Barbara's call to action for the Maple View principals generated analysis and examination that resulted in an acute awareness of unsuccessful results for some student groups. Unwilling to accept these outcomes as "predictable patterns of failure," Barbara envisioned a different future in which every student would achieve success. To achieve her vision required culturally proficient leadership that challenged the people in her organization to change and supported them in accomplishing the change. She created the infrastructure, conditions, and opportunities for personal and organizational learning through which knowledge, meaning, and purpose became unified in the goal of being culturally proficient.

The intent of this book is twofold: to inspire you to take on Barbara's challenge as your own personal goal and to provide you with the information and tools to achieve that goal. Culturally proficient leadership happens every day in the choices and decisions an individual makes. When you choose to question your assumptions, change your attitude, and redefine your purpose, you are embarking on a journey of personal transformation. To become culturally proficient, you make the choice to question your assumptions: You face your own anger, guilt, racism, or privilege. Leadership requires you to engage others in facing the challenge of becoming culturally proficient. At its very essence, culturally proficient leadership involves assuming responsibility for challenging and supporting others to question their values, change their perspectives, and develop new ways of behaving. This view of leadership relies on facilitating learning, knowledge building, and shared commitment to making things better. The choice to lead is yours.

Maple View Case Study Characters

Character	Role	Chapter(s)
Dr. Jack Bradley	Hospital CEO	1
Dr. James Harris	Director of Academic Programs, Tri-Cities Community College	1
Dr. Barbara Campbell	Superintendent	1–7
Dr. Charles Banks	School improvement coach	2
Sam Brewer	Principal, Pine Hills High School (PHHS)	2–4
Rob Moore	Teacher, PHHS	2, 4
Joel Peters	Teacher, PHHS	2, 4
Rose Diaz-Harris	Vice Principal, Maple View Elementary School (MVES)	2
Connie Barkley	Third-grade teacher, MVES	2, 5
Joan Stephens	Fifth-grade teacher, MVES	2, 5
Dr. Stephanie Barnes	School improvement coach, PHHS	2
Jack Thompson	Science teacher, PHHS	2, 4
Janice Thompson	School counselor, PHHS	2, 4
Maxine Parks	English teacher, PHHS	2
Ed Johnson	Principal, MVES	2
Janice Ross	Principal, neighboring district	2
Jim Jones	Physical education teacher/coach, PHHS	2
Alice Falls	History teacher, PHHS	2
Dr. Jesse Phillips	Author	2
Bob Moore	Sixth-grade teacher, Maple View Middle School (MVMS)	2
Laura Alvarez	Assistant Principal, MVES	2

Dr. Belinda Jackson	District math specialist	2
Ella Chapman	Parent, Maple View Arts (MVA)	2
Gregory Chapman	Parent, MVA	2
Anh Me Vu	Parent, MVA	2
Dr. Andrew Ramsey	Facilitator	2
Dr. Frederick Jackson	Facilitator	2
Tony Franklin	Principal, Pine Hills Middle School	2, 3
Dr. Frank Johnson	Educational administration professor, Midland State University (MSU)	2
Jung Hai	Graduate student, MSU	2
Jorge Alvarenga	Graduate student, MSU	2
Dr. Alfredo Crawford	English language acquisition consultant	3
Ira Robinson	Math teacher, MVMS	3
Dr. Laura Ruiz	Reading consultant	3
Anne Browning	District reading consultant	3
Dorothy Jackson	Teacher, MVES	3
Maureen Bailey	Principal, Rose Garden Elementary School (RGES)	3
Maxine Cho	Teacher, RGES	3
Dr. Connie Hampton	Principal, Maple View High School (MVHS)	3
Josh Turner	Biology teacher, MVHS	3
Irene Thompson	Counselor, MVHS	3
Helene Kim	History teacher, seventh grade, MVMS	3
Jackie Sims	Social studies teacher, sixth grade, MVMS	3
Francisco Alvarado	Assistant Principal, MVMS	3
Lucy Tyrell	Counselor, MVMS	3
Kwame Randolph	Parent, MVMS	3
Sarah Chainey	Science teacher, sixth grade, MVMS	3
Ron Paige	Algebra teacher, eighth grade, MVMS	3
Jocelyn Donaldson	Language arts teacher, seventh grade, MVMS	3
Gary Thompson	Mayor, Maple View	7
Oscar Medina	Principal, MVHS	2, 7

References

Argyris, Chris. (1990). *Overcoming organizational defenses: Facilitating organizational learning.* Needham, MA: Allyn & Bacon.

Argyris, Chris, & Schon, Donald A. (1974). *Theory in practice.* San Francisco: Jossey-Bass.

Argyris, Chris, & Schon, Donald A. (1996). *Organizational learning* (Vol. 2). San Francisco: Jossey-Bass.

Banks, James. (1999). *An introduction to multicultural education* (3rd ed.). Needham, MA: Addison-Wesley.

Block, Peter. (2001). *The answer to how is yes.* San Francisco: Berrett-Koehler.

Bohm, David. (1996). *On dialogue.* New York: Routledge.

Bohn, Anita Petra, & Sleeter, Christine E. (2000). Multicultural education and the standards movement: A report from the field. *Kappan, 82*(2), 156–159.

Brown, John Seely, & Duguid, Paul. (2000). *The social life of information.* Cambridge, MA: Harvard Business School Press.

Brown, Juanita S., & Isaacs, David. (2001, June/July). The world café: Living knowledge through conversations that matter. *The Systems Thinker,* 1–5.

Costa, Art L., & Garmston, Robert J. (2002). *Cognitive coaching: A foundation for renaissance schools* (2nd ed.). Norwood, MA: Christopher-Gordon.

Covey, Stephen R. (1989). *The seven habits of highly effective people.* New York: Fireside.

Cross, Terry L. (1989). *Toward a culturally competent system of care.* Washington, DC: Georgetown University Child Development Program, Child and Adolescent Service System Program.

Cross, Terry L., Bazron, Barbara J., Dennis, Karl W., & Isaacs, Mareasa R. (1993). *Toward a culturally competent system of care* (Vol. 2). Washington, DC: Georgetown University Child Development Program, Child and Adolescent Service System Program.

Delpit, Lisa. (1995). *Other people's children.* New York: New Press.

Elmore, Richard. (2000). *Building a new structure for school leadership.* Washington, DC: Albert Shanker Institute.

Freire, Paolo. (1970). *Pedagogy of the oppressed* (Nyra Bergman Ramos, Trans.). New York: Seabury.

Freire, Paolo. (1987). *Pedagogy of the oppressed.* New York: Continuum.

Freire, Paulo. (1999). *Pedagogy of hope: Reliving pedagogy of the oppressed.* New York: Continuum.

Fullan, Michael. (1991). *The new meaning of educational change.* New York: Teachers College Press.

Fullan, Michael. (2003). *The moral imperative of school leadership.* Thousand Oaks, CA: Corwin Press.

Gandhi, Mohandas K. (2002). Available at http://www.mahatma.org.

Garcia, Eugene. (1999). *Student cultural diversity: Understanding and meeting the challenge.* Boston: Houghton Mifflin.

Gladwell, Malcolm. (2000). *The tipping point: How little things can make a big difference.* Boston: Little, Brown.

Goleman, Daniel. (1995). *Emotional intelligence.* New York: Bantam.

Gollnick, Donna M., & Chinn, Philip C. (1990). *Multicultural education in a pluralistic society.* Englewood Cliffs, NJ: Prentice Hall.

Gordon, Milton M. (1964). *Assimilation in American life: The role of race, religion, and national origins.* New York: Oxford University Press.

Graham, Stephanie, & Lindsey, Randall B. (2002, March/April). Balance of power. *Leadership,* 20–23.

Hargrove, Robert. (1999). *Masterful coaching.* Available at http://www.rhargrove.com.

Heifetz, Ronald A. (1994). *Leadership without easy answers.* Cambridge, MA: Belknap.

Hilliard, Asa. (1991). Do we have the will to educate all children? *Educational Leadership, 40*(1), 31–36.

Kovel, Joel. (1984). *White racism: A psychohistory.* New York: Columbia University Press.

Ladson-Billings, Gloria. (1994). *The dreamkeepers: Successful teachers of African-American children.* San Francisco: Jossey-Bass.

Lindsey, Randall B. (2001, Fall). Diversity and professors of educational leadership: Political correctness or a core part of our curriculum? *Educational Leadership and Administration: Teaching and Program Development, 13,* 15–24.

Lindsey, Randall B., Nuri Robins, K., & Terrell, Raymond D. (1999). *Cultural proficiency: A manual for school leaders.* Thousand Oaks, CA: Corwin.

Lindsey, Randall B., Nuri Robins, K., & Terrell, Raymond D. (2003). *Cultural proficiency: A manual for school leaders* (2nd ed.). Thousand Oaks, CA: Corwin.

Loewen, James. (1995). *Lies my teacher told me: Everything your American history textbook got wrong.* New York: New Press.

Maeroff, Gene. (1999). *Altered destinies: Making life better for school children in need.* New York: St. Martin's.

Maturana, Humberto, & Varela, Francisco. (1992). *The tree of knowledge: The biological roots of human understanding.* Boston: Shambhala.

Myrdal, Gunnar. (1944). *An American dilemma: The Negro problem and modern democracy.* New York: Pantheon.

Nieto, Sonia. (2000). *Affirming diversity: The sociopolitical context of multicultural education* (3rd ed.). Reading, MA: Addison-Wesley.

Nuri Robins, K., Lindsey, Randall B., Lindsey, Delores B., & Terrell, Raymond D. (2002). *Culturally proficient instruction: A guide for people who teach.* Thousand Oaks, CA: Corwin.

Ogbu, John. (1992). Understanding cultural diversity and learning. *Educational Researcher, 21*(8), 5–14.

Owens, Robert G. (1995). *Organizational behavior in education* (5th ed.). Boston: Allyn & Bacon.

Reeves, Douglas B. (2000). *Accountability in action: A blueprint for learning organizations.* Denver, CO: Center for Performance Assessment.

Schein, Edgar H. (1992). *Organizational culture and leadership.* San Francisco: Jossey-Bass.

Schon, Donald A. (1987). *Educating the reflective practitioner: Toward a new design for teaching and learning in the professions.* San Francisco: Jossey-Bass.

Schwartz, Theodore. (1978). Where is the culture? Personality as the distributive locus of culture. In George D. Spinder (Ed.), *The making of psychological culture* (pp. 419–441). Berkeley: University of California Press.

Senge, Peter. (1994). *The fifth discipline fieldbook.* New York: Doubleday.

Sergiovanni, Thomas J. (1992). *Moral leadership: Getting to the heart of school improvement.* New York: Jossey-Bass.

Sheets, Rosa Hernandez. (2000). Advancing the field or taking center stage: The white movement in multicultural education. *Educational Researcher, 29*(9), 15–20.

Suarez-Orozco, Marcelo M. (1985, May). *Opportunity, family dynamics, and school achievement: The sociocultural context of motivation among recent immigrants from Central America.* Paper presented at the University of California Symposium on Linguistics, Minorities, and Education. In Garcia, E. (Ed.). (1999). *Student cultural diversity: Understanding and meeting the challenge* (2nd ed., pp. 45–146). Boston: Houghton Mifflin.

Tatum, Beverly Daniel. (1999). *Why are all the black kids sitting together in the cafeteria?* New York: Basic Books.

Terry, Robert. (1970). *For whites only.* Grand Rapids, MI: Eerdmans.

Weick, Karl E. (1979). *The social psychology of organizing* (2nd ed.). New York: McGraw Hill.

Wenger, Etienne. (1998). *Communities of practice: Learning, meaning, and identity.* Cambridge, UK: Cambridge University Press.

Wenger, Etienne C., & Snyder, W. M. (2000, January/February). Communities of practice: The organizational frontier. *Harvard Business Review,* 139–145.

Wheatley, Margaret J. (1992). *Leadership and the new science.* San Francisco: Berrett-Koehler.

Wheatley, Margaret J. (2002). *Turning to one another: Simple conversations to restore hope to the future.* San Francisco: Berrett-Koehler.

Zander, Benjamin, & Zander, Rosamund Stone. (2000). *The art of possibility: Transforming professional and personal and personal life.* Cambridge, MA: Harvard Business School Press.

Bibliography

Argyris, Chris. (1982). *Reasoning, learning, and action.* San Francisco: Jossey-Bass.

Argyris, Chris. (1992, Winter). Why individuals and organizations have difficulty in double-loop learning. *Organizational Dynamics, 7–38.*

Argyris, Chris. (1993). *Knowledge for action: A guide to overcoming barriers to organizational change.* San Francisco: Jossey-Bass.

Cheek, Robert. (1976). *Assertive black puzzled white.* San Luis Obispo, CA: Impact.

Coburn, Cynthia E. (2003). Rethinking scale: Moving beyond numbers to deep and lasting change. *Educational Researcher, 32*(6), 3–12.

Finn, Patrick J. (1999). *Literacy with an attitude: Educating working-class children in their own self-interest.* Albany: State University of New York Press.

Gordon, Milton M. (1978). *Human nature, class, and ethnicity.* New York: Oxford University Press.

Hargrove, Robert. (1995). *Masterful coaching: Extraordinary results by impacting people and the way they think and work together.* San Francisco: Jossey-Bass.

Kim, Daniel H. (1991, September). Systemic quality management: Improving the quality of doing and thinking. *The Systems Thinker, 3.*

Kuhn, Thomas S. (1962). *The structure of scientific revolutions.* Chicago: University of Chicago Press.

Lewis, Amanda E. (2001). There is no "race" in the schoolyard: Color-blind ideology in an (almost) all-white school. *American Educational Research Journal, 38*(4), 781–811.

Lipman, Pauline. (1998). *Race, class, and power in school restructuring.* Albany: State University of New York Press.

McAllister, Gretchen, & Irvine, Jacqueline Jordan. (2000). Cross cultural competency and multicultural teacher education. *Review of Educational Research, 70*(1), 3–24.

McCarthy, Cameron, & Crichlow, Warren. (Eds.). (1993). *Race identity and representation in education.* New York: Routledge.

McIntyre, Alice M. (1997). *Making meaning of whiteness: Exploring racial identity with white teachers.* Albany: State University of New York Press.

Ortiz, Ann M., Rhoads, Robert A., Mina, Liliana, & Hornak, Anne. (2000, April). *Deconstructing whiteness as part of a framework for multicultural education.* Workshop presented at the American College Personnel Association, Washington, DC.

Peterkin, Robert S., & Jackson, Janice. (2001). Racism, belief systems and student achievement. *Education Week, 21*(5), 21.

Pollock, Mica. (2001). How the question we ask most about race in education is the very question we most suppress. *Educational Researcher, 30*(9), 2–12.

Reeves, Douglas B. (2002). *Holistic accountability: Serving students, schools, and community.* Thousand Oaks, CA: Corwin.

Riehl, Carolyn J. (2000). The principal's role in creating inclusive schools for diverse students: A review of normative, empirical, and critical literature on the practice of educational administration. *Review of Educational Research, 70*(1), 55–81.

Schacter, Daniel. (2002). *The seven sins of memory: How the mind forgets and remembers.* Boston: Houghton Mifflin.

Schein, Edgar H. (1999). *The corporate culture survival guide: Sense and nonsense about culture change.* San Francisco: Jossey-Bass.

Stepsis, JoAnn. (1981). Communication styles. In J. W. Pfeiffer & J. Jones (Eds.), *1981 annual handbook for group facilitators.* San Diego: University Associates.

Index

**CORWIN
PRESS**

The Corwin Press logo—a raven striding across an open book—represents the union of courage and learning. Corwin Press is committed to improving education for all learners by publishing books and other professional development resources for those serving the field of K–12 education. By providing practical, hands-on materials, Corwin Press continues to carry out the promise of its motto: **"Helping Educators Do Their Work Better."**